# The Wisdom of Tolerance

**Abdurrahman Wahid** (1940–2009) served between 1999 and 2001 as the first democratically elected President of Indonesia. Advocate of a liberal, reforming Islam, he was throughout his career a champion of peace and interfaith dialogue, calling for people of all religions to work together against hatred and extremism.

**Daisaku Ikeda** (1928–) is President of Soka Gakkai International, a Buddhist network that actively promotes peace, culture, and education, whose members come from over 190 countries worldwide. He is the author of more than 100 books on Buddhist themes, and received the United Nations Peace Award in 1983.

# The Wisdom of Tolerance

## A Philosophy of Generosity and Peace

### Abdurrahman Wahid and Daisaku Ikeda

I.B. TAURIS

LONDON · NEW YORK

Published in 2015 by
I.B.Tauris & Co. Ltd
London • New York
www.ibtauris.com

Original Copyright © 2009 Abdurrahman Wahid and Daisaku Ikeda
English Translation Copyright © 2015 Soka Gakkai

The right of Abdurrahman Wahid and Daisaku Ikeda to be identified as the authors
of this work has been asserted by the authors in accordance with the Copyright,
Designs and Patents Act 1988.

References to websites were correct at the time of writing.

ISBN (HB): 978 1 78453 091 4
ISBN (PB): 978 1 78453 092 1
eISBN: 978 0 85773 963 6

A full CIP record for this book is available from the British Library
A full CIP record is available from the Library of Congress

Library of Congress Catalog Card Number: available

Typeset by Initial Typesetting Services, Edinburgh
Printed and bound in Great Britain by T.J. International, Padstow, Cornwall

# Contents

# Foreword by Shinta Nuriyah Wahid

First, let me take this opportunity to send peaceful greetings to all of you. May the One Almighty God have mercy and shower His blessings upon all of us.

As the wife of KH Abdurrahman Wahid, I truly understood my husband's sincere desire to convey philosophies of peace and policies that promote tolerance for global citizens. During his life, Gus Dur (my husband's moniker) had met Dr Daisaku Ikeda, with whom he had talks about diverse issues, mainly about efforts toward realizing better global communities.

Gus Dur had also read the dialogue between Arnold Toynbee and Daisaku Ikeda, which he found very inspirational, and since then, he had always wanted to meet the two individuals. In 2002, Gus Dur paid Dr Ikeda a visit in Japan. Our daughter, Anita, and I came along, accompanying him on the trip. Although it was his first time meeting Dr Ikeda, Gus Dur felt as if he had met a good friend whom he hadn't seen for a long time. Both men spoke with each other in an amicable way, and each was able to comprehensively recognize the noble tasks they needed to undertake. And for this purpose, the two men set their hearts on answering today's global challenges through *The Wisdom of Tolerance*.

It would certainly take a long time to finish such an extensive dialogue, one that would be valuable for humanity. In addition, due to the great distance between Indonesia and Japan, it was also impossible for the two men to always meet face to face; however, they overcame that problem by continuing their dialogue through correspondence and recordings.

Gus Dur realized that this brilliant exchange of thoughts and ideas had to be developed constantly and progressively, especially for future generations. For that reason, they structured their dialogue in a way to allow readers to grasp the significance of tolerance for the sake of peace and civilization. This dialogue between these two men represents peace and harmony between two countries with different backgrounds, be they cultural, linguistic, or religious. Yet they also believed that with total commitment, probity, and deep sincerity, we will be able to create a harmonious and peaceful life in the truest sense.

*The Wisdom of Tolerance* abounds with thoughts and ideas for the benefit of humanity, especially for those generations that are to follow. Accordingly, Gus Dur hoped that this book would be translated into many different languages, so that it could be enjoyed by anyone who cares about peace and harmony. Dr Ikeda's books have been translated into forty-five languages and published worldwide. Among them, the Indonesian edition of *The Wisdom of Tolerance* has become a bestseller in Indonesia.

Last but not least, on behalf of KH Abdurrahman Wahid's family, I would like to take this opportunity to give my most heartfelt thanks and show my deepest appreciation to Dr Ikeda and Soka Gakkai – both have helped fulfil my husband's hope; that is, to publish this book in many languages. May the One and Almighty God bless such a noble and sincere effort, and protect all of us, always. Amen.

Dra. Hj. Shinta Nuriyah Wahid, M. Hum
Jakarta, 18 November 2014

# ONE

# The Mission of All Religions – Peace

**Daisaku Ikeda:** New value is created through encounters between individuals, and new chapters of history are written through exchanges between civilizations.

I am truly delighted to have this opportunity to speak with and learn from such an eminent sage, philosopher, and man of religious conviction as you, President Wahid.

I am joined by people in various circles throughout Japanese society who are eagerly looking forward to our dialogue, seeing it as an exchange of peace and culture bringing together Islam and Buddhism.

**Abdurrahman Wahid:** I have known of you, President Ikeda, from about 1980.

I have wanted to meet and speak with you since reading *Choose Life*,[1] your dialogue with the British historian Arnold J. Toynbee (1889–1975). The opportunity has arrived at last.

**Ikeda:** I am sure Dr Toynbee would be pleased to hear you say that. He had visited Indonesia and highly admired your people and nation, which he praised as a place where differing religions coexisted amicably.[2]

He also wrote: 'In this vital matter of religious tolerance, Indonesia has set an example that the rest of us would do well to follow.'[3]

Of the 230 million people living in Indonesia, nearly 90 per cent are followers of Islam, making it the country with the largest Muslim population in the world.

1

At the same time, various other religions, including Buddhism, Hinduism, and Christianity, coexist peacefully with Islam in Indonesia.

In that harmonious setting, you are one of your nation's pre-eminent leaders. You not only serve as the president of the largest Muslim organization in Indonesia, the Nahdlatul Ulama (NU), and stand tall as a giant of culture and learning, you were also the wise and able President of the Republic of Indonesia.

This opportunity to engage in dialogue with you and absorb your enlightening insights is a precious treasure, not only for me, but also for the young people of our future.

**Wahid:** You, too, are a great man, President Ikeda. You uplift humanity through the power of culture. You are a seeker of the human spirit who has elevated humankind to a new level.

You have also, in our increasingly materialistic global culture, revived the philosophy of Buddhism with its rich humanism.

I hope to nurture our friendship and continue building upon the ties that we share.

**Ikeda:** Thank you for your kind words.

You have previously engaged in dialogues with representatives of both Christianity and Judaism.

I have also striven to meet with numerous individuals in an effort to promote dialogue among civilizations and religions on a person-to-person basis.

I believe there is a wise saying in Indonesia, 'If you lose your way, go back to the starting point.'

The founder and first president of Soka Gakkai, Tsunesaburo Makiguchi (1871–1944), who gave his life for his commitment to peace, also frequently said: 'If you become deadlocked, return to the prime point!'

What is the starting point, the prime point, to which humankind needs to return at this moment in our history?

It is peace. All religions should work together in the service of peace.

The purpose of religion is human happiness. Though their specific doctrines may differ, all religions can cooperate for the sake of the peace of humanity. This is the central theme that I wish to pursue with you, President Wahid.

Previously, in an historic and brilliant speech, you stated that as the

United Nations enters the twenty-first century, it should call on the entire world to engage in dialogue.

**Wahid:** Thank you. I gave that speech at the United Nations Millennium Summit in 2000. I expressed my conviction that dialogue can provide a human face regardless of ethnicity, cultural differences or historical backgrounds and pave the way for promotion of common values and a commitment for a global culture of peace and harmony.

This is something we in Indonesia know from personal experience.

**Ikeda:** I agree wholeheartedly.

As you noted, there is only one basic path to take as we set forth into the new millennium and that is to engage in a discourse for peace.

**Wahid:** I support the nonviolent ideals of Mahatma Gandhi (1869–1948). As I have asserted, Islam itself doesn't advocate war; rather, it is people who wage war.

At present, through the activities of the Wahid Institute, we are working to promote the harmonious coexistence of different religions and win broader acceptance of cultural diversity.

I continue to speak in the United States and many other countries and conduct various efforts to cultivate a correct understanding of Islam.

We also sponsor international conferences in which Islamic leaders from around the world participate, in order to correct the mistaken image of Islam that tends to predominate in the Western countries.

**Ikeda:** Yes, I am aware of your activities.

The fact is that most people in Japan still know very little about Islam.

I have published a dialogue with the Iranian peace scholar Majid Tehranian (1937–2012), *Global Civilization: A Buddhist–Islamic Dialogue.*

In our dialogue, Dr Tehranian stressed that the word 'Islam' can be traced etymologically to the word for peace.

**Wahid:** Yes, that's absolutely correct.

**Ikeda:** Buddhism, which upholds the worth and dignity of life, is also absolutely committed to peace – a commitment it shares with Islam.

**Wahid:** And the aim of our dialogue between Islam and Buddhism is also peace.

**Ikeda:** Yes. I would like to join you in exploring the philosophy of peace and the wisdom of tolerance.

I am equally motivated by the wish to strengthen and expand the friendship between our two nations.

Indonesia has a tradition of respecting cultural diversity, and will play a crucial role in Asia in the twenty-first century. In terms of population, too, it is one of the largest countries in the world, following China, India, and the United States.

It is also the Islamic country that the Japanese people feel most familiar with.

We have enduring ties, and have had official diplomatic relations for fifty years.

In 2008, the Japanese Ministry of Land, Infrastructure, Transport and Tourism published a satisfaction index of Japanese tourists who travelled abroad, with Indonesia beating all other countries as the most satisfying overseas destination.

**Wahid:** I'm happy to hear that.

I have visited Japan more than ten times, and I am very fond of your country.

**Ikeda:** Dr Toynbee once wrote, 'Such glimpses of the real world are gleanings of priceless value.'[4]

Far too often, we judge other countries based on preconceived notions and prejudices. Dr Toynbee and I agreed that the way to dispel such misunderstandings and misperceptions is for the people of different countries to communicate more freely with and learn from one another.

Like Japan, Indonesia is an island nation, though it is very different in many respects. For example, Indonesia has five times the landmass of Japan, and the distance it stretches from east to west is comparable to the distance from the east to the west coast of the United States. Japan has some 7,000 islands, but Indonesia is the world's largest 'archipelago nation', with more than 17,000 islands.

More than 300 ethnic groups coexist peacefully in Indonesia, endowing your nation with a very rich culture.

Indonesia also differs greatly from Japan in its climate and topography.

**Wahid:** Sitting directly beneath the equator, the natural environment of Indonesia appears to be very attractive to the Japanese.

Japan has four distinct seasons, but Indonesia has two – the rainy season and the dry season.

The rich cultural variety of Indonesia also appeals greatly to Japanese people.

I also think that the friendliness and warmth of the Indonesian people makes a favourable impression on visitors to our country.

**Ikeda:** Yes, I agree.

The warmth and hospitality of the Indonesian people is truly a marvel.

Indonesia is blessed by a profusion of such lush and beautiful flowers as the hibiscus, bougainvillea, orchids, and night-blooming cereus; it is also home to the world's largest flower, Rafflesia.

**Wahid:** In Indonesia the arrival of the rainy season is heralded by the blossoming of the flame tree (Flamboyant). Its scarlet flowers bloom in the hottest season, and when they fall and new leaves sprout on the trees, the rainy season begins.

In Japan, the cherry blossoms are the harbingers of spring.

**Ikeda:** Yes, the cherry blossom is Japan's national flower. I have loved cherry blossoms since I was a boy.

Your national flower is the jasmine *(melati)*, isn't it?

**Wahid:** Yes. I love jasmine flowers. From the time I was little, we were told that jasmine flowers are the flowers of *wali*, a sacred protector in Islam. The blossoms are small and white and have a very distinctive fragrance.

**Ikeda:** I have been told that a Javanese proverb observes, 'The jasmine flower grows where a person of pure heart resides.'

The jasmine flower is indeed an appropriate symbol of the people of Indonesia.

Nichiren (1222–82), whose Buddhist teachings we members of Soka

Gakkai International follow, wrote: 'If the minds of living beings are impure, their land is also impure, but if their minds are pure, so is their land.'[5]

Pure minds spawn a pure land in which nature is protected and shines with beauty.

**Wahid:** I recall attending the exhibition of your photographs, 'Dialogue with Nature', held in Jakarta in 2007. I am deeply grateful for that fine exhibition you presented in our country. The theme of 'dialogue with nature' is very important.

God gave humankind nature to use in the best possible way.

As such, if humankind does nothing for nature, it means we have abandoned and are harming nature.

Harming nature is the same as harming our own humanity.

Islam has a wonderful saying – 'The God is within oneself.'

Nature is very close and important to us, and as such we must always protect it.

**Ikeda:** That is very true. In addition, I remain deeply grateful to you for your generous assistance on the occasion of the exhibition, which was vital to its success.

Shakyamuni included the jasmine among the most ambrosial of flowers, saying that a person of virtue exceeds even the jasmine flower in fragrance: 'The odour of the flower travels not against the wind, nor does that of aloe-wood, of incense, or of chandana. The odour of the holy travels even against the wind; all regions are pervaded by the fragrance of the perfect man.'[6]

The perfume of one's virtuous character imparts hope and courage to others, not only when circumstances are favourable, but also when they are not. I find this simile closely consonant with you and your life, President Wahid, for you have striven mightily to overcome various difficulties to lead your people to peace and prosperity.

**Wahid:** You are too kind. To be honest, I never regarded difficulties as difficulties.

When I lost most of my sight, as well as when I experienced a serious illness the year before I became my nation's president, my only thought was to accept what God had given me.

At the same time, I determined to do my best in my new circumstances.

I have never once lamented my destiny. I have used whatever has befallen me in life as a motivation to strive my hardest each day to continue with my work.

**Ikeda:** I find your resolve profoundly moving.

I myself have been the target of vitriol and maltreatment on numerous occasions, but I have always pressed ahead, regarding the criticism and unjust acts against me that result from my commitment to peace and justice as an honour.

From my youth, I have encouraged myself with the mottoes, 'The strong man is strongest when alone'[7] and 'The greater the resistance met by waves, the stronger they surge.'

I understand that you were also the target of unpardonable abuse as a man who stayed true to his beliefs and as a man who strives to better the lives of his people in the world of politics.

Have you ever been betrayed and left embittered by it?

**Wahid:** I have been so frequently betrayed that I am no longer disturbed by the experience.

But most importantly, I have learned something from each such event.

In July 2001, after I stepped down as president, I announced that I would continue to work for democracy. I had no regrets then, either.

My only sadness at leaving the presidential palace was that in the process I somehow lost some of my favourite tapes of Beethoven's music.

**Ikeda:** You are indeed a person who has successfully managed to transform adversity into fuel for further advances.

I first met you in April 2002, a year after your term as president had ended.

I recall thinking that your clear, strong voice rang with conviction.

**Wahid:** I was tremendously inspired and encouraged by our meeting in Tokyo. It led me to renew my pledge to devote the rest of my life to Indonesia.

**Ikeda:** You are too generous.

Ludwig van Beethoven (1770–1827), whom you just mentioned, once declared: 'I will seize fate by the throat; it shall certainly never wholly overcome me. Oh! Life is so beautiful, would I could have a thousand lives!'[8]

Beethoven has always been a great source of inspiration and encouragement for me, particularly in that he succeeded in giving us such immortal masterpieces as Symphony No. 5, Symphony No. 9, with its 'Ode to Joy', and other works in spite of the great tribulations he faced.

I have fond memories of listening with friends as a young man to Beethoven on an old gramophone, the triumphant sound of his music nourishing our souls and rousing our courage.

**Wahid:** I especially love Beethoven's Ninth Symphony: it reflects his life, filled with such turbulent changes and struggles.

The theme, pressing onward through suffering to joy, is surely a reflection of his own experience in composing the symphony.

By that time he had already completely lost his hearing.

That is precisely why he was able to compose such a lofty and moving choral section, leading listeners to praise it as a 'voice surpassing human wisdom.'

**Ikeda:** It is indeed a timeless work.

Great art ascends to the heights of religious awe. At the same time, the latter serves as a profound source for the creation of the former.

And true art entails the most exalted anguish, and is accompanied by the joy and exultation attained when transcending that anguish. It offers people faith and love achieved through the sublimation of the artist's personal struggles.

I believe that is why such art is able to transcend the ages, transcend nationality, to touch and move the lives of those who lead their lives in an earnest, thoughtful manner.

'Art,' as Beethoven famously said, 'unites everybody.'[9]

Music, the unsullied flower found in every country, in every culture and among every people, has the power to bring all of us together.

**Wahid:** Yes. I still remember how the students at Soka University welcomed me with a performance on the traditional Japanese stringed instrument, the *koto*, when I visited.

At the Min-On Concert Association, I was able to hear the sound of an heirloom piano of the type that Wolfgang Amadeus Mozart (1756–91) favoured and Beethoven praised. I also had the opportunity to hear the piece 'Mother', for which you composed the lyrics. One of the women working there sang an a cappella rendition of it for me.

The melody was lovely in itself, but when I heard the meaning of the lyrics, I was deeply moved. I was presented with a CD of the song recorded by various artists, and I listened to it immediately upon returning to my hotel room.

**Ikeda:** I am honoured. The Min-On Concert Association, which has celebrated its forty-sixth anniversary in 2009, has sponsored performances and artistic exchanges with more than 100 countries and territories.

I am happy to say that since sponsoring performances in Japan of Indonesia's oldest traditional dance troupe, the Siswa Among Beksa of Yogyakarta Royal Palace, in 1973, Min-On has been able to bring numerous outstanding Indonesian performing artists to audiences in cities throughout Japan, including a traditional drama and dance troupe sent by the Indonesian government, the Gentra Madya Art Troupe, the Pelangi Nusantara Dance Troupe of Taman Mini Indonesia Indah, and the Kabumi Art Troupe.

Traditional Javanese dance and gamelan music are admired and appreciated around the world.

At the 1889 World's Fair in Paris, four female Javanese dancers and a gamelan orchestra caused quite a stir.

The French composer Claude Debussy (1862–1918) held Javanese music in high esteem, and his attempts to incorporate certain elements of it in his own compositions and open up new creative directions in music are well known.

Japan and the rest of the world have much to learn from Indonesia and its rich and vibrantly creative artistic heritage.

**Wahid:** The amicable relationship between Japan and Indonesia should be of benefit to both nations. In other words, there is much that Indonesia can learn from the Japanese people, and naturally the reverse is equally true.

I personally am very fond of Japanese culture.

From my youth I loved films, and the works of director Akira Kurosawa (1910–98) are among some of my favourites.

I have seen almost all of Kurosawa's films, from his iconic *Seven Samurai* (1954) to his last work, *Rhapsody in August* (1991).

**Ikeda:** Kurosawa wanted to build peace through culture.

He once said that those involved in creating works of art are probably the best suited for building a movement for world peace. Their sensitivity, imagination, and respect for culture, he suggested, make it easier for them to understand others.

Toshiro Mifune (1920–97), who appeared in sixteen of Kurosawa's films, including *Seven Samurai, High and Low* (1963) and *Red Beard* (1965), was a close friend. His daughter is also in the arts, an actress.

I am certain that Mr Mifune would have been very happy to learn that such a world-renowned man of culture as you, President Wahid, appreciates Kurosawa's films.

Indonesia also has a rich literary heritage. Pramoedya Ananta Toer (1925–2006), for example, is known as one of Indonesia's greatest modern writers.

**Wahid:** Yes. He was in fact a dear friend of mine.

On his seventieth birthday, I went to his home and we had a photograph taken together.

In the political climate of the time, having a photograph taken with Pramoedya required courage, particularly for an Indonesian.

He warned me that if I had a photograph taken with him, the state intelligence agency would report it to the military.

And he added that he bet I must have seen people who appeared to be cigarette salesmen about every five metres along the large road to his house, explaining that they were all actually with the secret police.

I replied that if that was the case, there was no point in trying to hide my visit now!

**Ikeda:** I can see that the two of you shared a deep and noble bond. That episode shines with your trust in one another.

I was deeply moved when I read Pramoedya's masterwork, *This Earth of Mankind*.

One passage in particular is still etched in my mind: 'Life can give everything to whoever tries to understand and is willing to receive new knowledge.'[10]

You have been an assiduous student since your youth. Are there any works of Japanese literature that you are especially fond of?

**Wahid:** I have read the novels of Yasunari Kawabata (1899–1972) and Yukio Mishima (1925–70).

I was particularly struck by how Kawabata, in a way similar to the films of Kurosawa, is able to beautifully depict contemporary life while preserving elements of the Japanese tradition.

**Ikeda:** I see. The accommodation of the traditional and the modern is a major challenge.

I was scheduled to meet with Mr Kawabata once, but unfortunately it did not work out. I met Mr Mishima in a hotel barbershop on one occasion.

Kawabata held that beauty is ageless and universal.

He also spoke of how Japan was able to assimilate the culture of Tang-dynasty China (618–907) in its own unique way to create the splendid culture of the Heian period (794–1185), establishing a distinctly Japanese aesthetic.

Cultures are enriched and find sources of fresh creativity through exchange and interaction with other cultures.

**Wahid:** People such as Akira Kurosawa and Yasunari Kawabata are famous cultural figures representing Japan, but you, too, President Ikeda, have dedicated yourself to creating a fusion of Eastern and Western cultures – a fact of which I am deeply appreciative.

Visiting Min-On showed me how deeply culture is rooted in the hearts of the Japanese people.

It broadcasts the message that the Japanese are a culture-loving people. I think that Soka Gakkai is playing an important part in implementing this mission.

And the cultural exchange that you are promoting does not benefit Japan alone. It is for all humankind. I would like to see the power of culture as a force to resist the wave of materialism inundating our world.

**Ikeda:** I appreciate your words of encouragement.

The starting point of our movement for peace, culture, and education based on the Buddhist humanism of Nichiren may be found with Tsunesaburo Makiguchi, Soka Gakkai's founder and first president.

At a time when the majority of intellectuals and media agencies, fearful of retribution, refused to speak up against the transgressions against peace and human rights by the forces of Japanese chauvinism and militarism, Mr Makiguchi and his disciple Josei Toda (1900–58), the second president of Soka Gakkai, refused to be intimidated by the militarist regime and their threats and never retreated from their firmly held convictions.

In time, the government intensified its oppression, with officers of the Special Higher Police following Makiguchi and the meetings he attended placed under surveillance, denying him the right to speak freely. In spite of that, he never wavered in his beliefs.

Eventually the authorities ordered the organization to cease publication of its journal, *Kachi Sozo* (Value Creation), and Makiguchi was arrested and imprisoned. Even as the authorities mercilessly sought his recantation, Makiguchi remained unbowed; after some 500 days as a prisoner of conscience, he died without ever regaining his freedom.

Makiguchi staunchly opposed the brutal fascist regime that invaded other Asian nations, opposing the war at the cost of his life.

Your grandfather, President Wahid, was severely beaten by Japanese soldiers during the Japanese occupation of Indonesia (1942–5), his right arm permanently disabled as a result.

**Wahid:** Yes. Many of those fighting for our nation's independence, including my grandfather KH Mohammad Hasyim Asy'ari (1871–1947), were arrested at that time.

My grandfather was a *kiai*, an expert in Islam. He was subjected to that brutal treatment because he refused to bow to the east, the direction of the rising sun, as a form of worship of the Japanese emperor.

**Ikeda:** As a Japanese, I offer you my deepest apologies.

The Japanese military invasion of Asia exacted an incalculable toll: countless Indonesians and other Asians were killed or had their lives shattered; unspeakable suffering was inflicted on millions of people.

During his interrogation in prison, Makiguchi spoke out against Japan's heinous deeds, declaring that its invasion of Asia was not the 'holy war' proclaimed by the Japanese government, and that a fundamental error in the national authorities' spiritual leadership had completely perverted Japan's actions.

In order to prevent a similar tragedy from ever occurring again, we have built and broadened our grassroots movement, carrying on Makiguchi's ideals and striving for world peace.

In addition, the institutions based on humanistic education I have founded, including the Soka schools and Soka University, have as their aim the fostering of individuals who will contribute to world peace.

**Wahid:** Several years ago, I invited a group of Soka University students visiting Indonesia to my home.

I shook hands with each of them, and sat for commemorative photographs with them. They were all wonderful students.

Hearing your account, I cannot help but reaffirm my feeling that Soka University produces such fine students precisely because its source is Makiguchi's peace philosophy.

**Ikeda:** As the university's founder, I would like to express my profound gratitude for the hospitality you so generously extended them. Our students were deeply moved by their meeting with you, and shared their joy at the experience with many.

We were also delighted to have your younger brother's daughter study at Soka University as an international student. I understand that she graduated in 2002 from the preparatory Japanese language programme with top honours.

Your younger brother has also taken the time to warmly encourage Soka University students. Please give him my best regards.

**Wahid:** I certainly will.

At present my nephew and his wife are living in Niigata because of his work. I am happy to say that my family's ties to Japan seem to be expanding year by year.

**Ikeda:** Niigata is Mr Makiguchi's birthplace.

He was born there in 1871, the same year as your grandfather's birth. It is indeed a serendipitous coincidence.

Makiguchi later moved to Hokkaido by himself, where he began his career as an educator.

Then he went to Tokyo, where he worked as an elementary school principal for many years, developing his pedagogical system of 'value creation' with the aim of empowering children to achieve their own happiness.

Our organization marks its inception with the publication of his groundbreaking work on education, *Soka Kyoikugaku Taikei* (The System of Value-Creating Pedagogy). At first it was an organization of mainly educators. In 2010, we celebrated our eightieth anniversary.

I have been told that your grandfather, who is revered as a national hero of the struggle for Indonesian independence, was also an eminent educator.

He was committed to introducing modern educational methods and subjects, including textbooks on such subjects as mathematics, science, and foreign languages that were considered progressive at the time.

**Wahid:** Yes, that's true.

My grandfather founded a *pesantren,* an Islamic boarding school, when he was twenty-eight.

Through the school he sought to elevate the moral and spiritual levels of the local community.

He built his school near a sugar factory operated by the Dutch.

At the time, there were many drinking and gambling establishments in the area, creating a very dubious moral climate.

But the residents depended upon the sugar factory for their livelihood, so there was nothing they could do. My grandfather wanted to change the situation through education.

He believed: 'If you can't change the fathers, change the mothers and children through education.'

**Ikeda:** That's a very perceptive insight. In many ways, mothers play a decisive role in families.

For the sake of the future, I think it is increasingly important to focus on the needs of mothers and children.

**Wahid:** The first thing my grandfather did was to create a *musholla sederhana,* a simple mosque. It was a very modest structure, made from bamboo. He allowed children to board there, protecting them from negative social influences and educating them.

Soon his school became well regarded as a centre of education in the community.

He introduced new and improved educational methods, which eventually spread to other *pesantren.*

At the time of his death, the school had grown to have a student body of 2,500.

Graduates went on to teach at other *pesantren* and open new schools of their own.

**Ikeda:** What an impressive life he lived.

The significance of the sacred task of education is that its light is passed from person to person until it grows into a force illuminating all of society.

Your grandfather was one of the founders of the Muslim organization Nahdlatul Ulama. He had supreme faith in education as a means to enlighten and empower people and treasured it above all else.

You have stressed the importance of elevating our humanity as well.

In the past you said that 'an important role of religion is to lift people out of poverty and servility.'

You have also called for the nurturing of a moral character that inspires people to see to it that those suffering in poverty are able to lead decent human lives, and to ensure that their fundamental human rights are respected. In Islam, you noted, morality means to sympathize with the plight of others.[11]

Your grandfather embodied those very convictions in his sublime life.

**Wahid:** I am delighted that you have correctly understood my grandfather and his life.

He was always tolerant and accepting of others, and I was profoundly influenced by his actions.

In Indonesian we have the word *santri*, meaning students at Islamic religious schools.

I learned from my grandfather's example the importance of maintaining an attitude of tolerance and acceptance, not only toward Islamic religious schools, but toward the activities of all organizations.

**Ikeda:** Your grandfather's spirit of tolerance and acceptance is manifested in Indonesia's official national motto, *Bhinneka Tunggal Ika* – Unity in Diversity.

**Wahid:** Yes. The tradition of diversity in Indonesia is summed up in the phrase of the great poet of the Majapahit Empire (1293–1518), Mpu Tantular, who lived in the fourteenth century: *Bhinneka Tunggal Ika*. In other words, though there is diversity, in essence all is one.

This idea that, though our opinions may differ, we are all in it together, has been fostered throughout Indonesia's history.

As a matter of fact, it was brought to Indonesia by the followers of Buddhism.

When the Chinese Buddhist monk I-Ching (Yijing; 635–713) promulgated Buddhism in Java during the Srivijaya Empire (683–1288), Indonesian religious teachings developed with great diversity.

15

As a result, our way of life, in which diversity is protected and upheld, can be seen as part of the Buddhist tradition introduced and developed by I-Ching.

**Ikeda:** I find that to be a very salient observation.

The Srivijaya Empire is known as a period in which the ancient Indonesian civilization flourished.

It was an important nexus along the trade routes linking China, India, and Ancient Rome.

Mahayana Buddhism also flourished there, and as a central hub for the dissemination of Buddhism, it was a meeting place of many cultures and peoples. Historical documents attest to its contacts with Nalanda, the Indian centre of Buddhist learning.

As one of the key points along the 'Maritime Silk Road', the Srivijaya Empire prospered for centuries.

Its glory and brilliance have fascinated many, not only historians.

Another great Indonesian kingdom, on a par with the Srivijaya Empire, was the Majapahit Empire.

**Wahid:** Yes, the Majapahit Empire was founded in 1293 by Raden Wijaya.

I believe that Raden Wijaya was actually of Chinese descent, probably a Chinese naval officer. Many in the Chinese navy at the time were members of the *tarekat* (or 'brotherhood', a group of Islamic mystics).

Under the protection of Chinese followers of Islam, the Majapahit Empire flourished as a state of diverse religions and ethnic groups.

With this diversity as its foundation, the Majapahit Empire survived for three centuries.

**Ikeda:** Diversity, when prized, serves as a source of dynamism and a driving force for prosperity. This is one of history's essential lessons.

In our subsequent discourse, I would like to shed further light on the history and tradition of your nation as a land that has woven together multiple cultures and served as a cradle fostering exchange, while examining what is needed to achieve peaceful coexistence in our world today.

**Wahid:** Yes.

I would also like to highlight the wisdom and historical lessons that can illuminate that purpose through our dialogue.

**Ikeda:** I am very fond of the Indonesian saying: 'There are no mountains too high to climb, no ravines too deep to descend, as long as there is a will.'

I have engaged in dialogue with people throughout the world with this same resolve.

Let us continue this discourse between Islam and Buddhism from a variety of perspectives for the sake of peace.

## TWO

# A Bridge of Friendship to the World

**Ikeda:** In July 2009, the oldest fragment of Islamic pottery discovered to date in Japan was unearthed in Nara Prefecture, the location of Japan's ancient capital, causing quite a stir.

It is believed that the vase from which the fragment comes was produced in a West Asian Islamic kingdom (the Abbasid Caliphate, 758–1258) in the second half of the eighth century, and brought to Japan through the 'Maritime Silk Road'.

When I was younger, I visited several of the countries that were once part of that great Islamic caliphate of the Middle East – Iran, Iraq, Turkey, and Egypt. That was in 1962, very soon after I had become the third president of Soka Gakkai.

This was at a time when few Japanese travelled overseas, and there was a high degree of prejudice against the countries of the Middle East.

I was convinced that for the sake of peace it was vital to reach out to the Islamic world and form bonds of friendship with Muslims.

I understand that you studied in the Middle East as a young man.

**Wahid:** Yes. In 1963, the year after your journey to the Middle East, I left my homeland to study overseas.

One of the places I studied was Al-Azhar University in Cairo, an eminent institution that has been a leader of scholarship in the Islamic world for a thousand years.

I mainly studied religion at the university, and it was there that

I learned for the first time that different interpretations of religious teachings exist, and indeed, are quite normal.

While experiencing the hallowed historic atmosphere of Cairo, I also gained a familiarity with the cultures of the United States and Europe. I particularly concentrated on reading literary classics, and I became an avid reader.

Books from cultures all over the world were available in Cairo, and I have fond memories of spending many fulfilling hours in the libraries of Cairo University and the American University in Cairo.

**Ikeda:** That was how your admirable record of higher learning began, then.

The Arabian language programme was established at Soka University in the year the school opened. Torao Kawasaki (1914–77),[1] a pioneer of Arabic studies in Japan, established the programme. Speaking of Islamic civilization, he often told his students: 'The differences in customs and manners are really minor. We're all human . . . You know that originally "Islam" also means "peace."'[2]

Professor Kawasaki also stressed that Islam, rather than being a religion of the desert, arose in the cities – crossroads through which people from many cultures passed.

Today, Soka University has research and academic ties with Cairo University and the American University in Cairo, where you spent time as a young man. We also have an active student exchange programme with both institutions.

Scholarly, educational, and cultural exchange help expand a universal network of humanity that transcends ethnic and religious boundaries.

**Wahid:** Yes, I agree.

The Prophet Mohammed (c.570–632) exhorted Muslims 'to seek knowledge even if it be in China.'[3]

At the time in the Arab world, China had the image of being the most faraway of all lands. Encouraging followers of Islam to seek wisdom even in such a distant place expresses an attitude of openness to other cultures and peoples.

**Ikeda:** Yes, I agree.

In the history of Buddhism, too, King Ashoka of India (304–232 BCE), for example, followed Shakyamuni's urging and sent emissaries to promote peaceful relations with such distant lands as Greece, Macedonia, Anatolia, Syria, Persia, and Egypt.

Soka University has academic relationships with more than a hundred universities around the world. In the Islamic world, they include universities not only in Indonesia and Egypt but in Turkey, Malaysia, and Brunei, among others.

I regard the students who come to study at Soka University from abroad as a treasure of the world and the future.

As the founder of Soka University, I have striven to encourage and look after our international students in the hope that they may focus on their studies and enjoy university life to the fullest, as well as to foster them as outstanding leaders who will continue contributing to world peace and the betterment of their respective societies.

**Wahid:** I have the highest hopes for exchange among students and young people for the sake of Indonesian–Japanese amity.

My sincere wish is that they will not become individuals who think solely of their self-interest but are concerned about the interests of society and act to promote world peace and harmony.

**Ikeda:** Those are my feelings exactly.

In June 2009, US President Barack Obama visited Egypt.

His lecture, jointly sponsored by Al-Azhar University and Cairo University, was received with considerable acclaim.

In it he urged the importance of dialogue and called for harmonious coexistence among civilizations, stressing the importance of building a new relationship with the Islamic world.

'Islam has a proud tradition of tolerance,'[4] he noted. 'I saw it first-hand as a child in Indonesia, where devout Christians worshiped freely in an overwhelmingly Muslim country. That is the spirit we need today.'[5]

While living in Indonesia, President Obama attended a school at which many of the students – his classmates and playmates – were Muslims. He experienced first-hand the tradition of acceptance and tolerance that informs Indonesian society.

That is what enabled him to attain a well-grounded view of Islam, without being influenced by prejudice and stereotypes.

**Wahid:** President Obama's speech was broadcast on television in Indonesia and also widely covered in the newspapers.

His emphasis on the spirit of tolerance and acceptance, and the importance of dialogue, are completely consonant with the views that I have stressed over the years. I think there is great significance in his promise as America's leader to strive to improve relations with the Islamic world.

**Ikeda:** In his speech, President Obama cited Indonesia as an example of freedom of belief, a crucial issue in our world.

I believe it was in fact none other than your father, Abdul Wahid Hasyim (1914–53), who strove so arduously to incorporate freedom of belief into Indonesia's constitution.

**Wahid:** Yes, that is correct.

From the time of the establishment of the Republic of Indonesia, my father was a minister, serving as the Minister of Religious Affairs three times.

In 1945, when our constitution was being drafted, there was vigorous debate over whether Islam should be designated as the national religion.

My father and others who shared his conviction argued the importance of respect for all religions, and language guaranteeing freedom of religious belief was incorporated into the constitution.

The position advocated by my father and others of like mind is now widely accepted throughout Indonesian society.

**Ikeda:** That is invaluable testimony, indeed.

The wise decision of your nation, with the largest Islamic population in the world, has global significance.

I was drawn to and admired the courage with which Indonesia stood up for its beliefs despite the Cold War tensions between the East and West following World War II.

First Indonesian President Sukarno (Kusno Sosrodihardjo, 1901–70) clearly stated his government's position of respecting all religions, declaring that the people of Indonesia were peerless when it came to their religious tolerance.

The contributions of your father and the other Indonesian leaders of the day in firmly establishing freedom of religious belief and a climate of religious tolerance and acceptance will shine for all time.

**Wahid:** Thank you.

My grandfather and father, who were both in positions of national leadership, supported President Sukarno and, based on their religious beliefs, acted wholeheartedly in the interests of the Indonesian people and Indonesia as a whole.

**Ikeda:** The year 2008 marked the sixtieth anniversary of the United Nations' adoption of the Universal Declaration of Human Rights.

The Third Committee drafting the Declaration consisted of members of various religious backgrounds who were among the foremost thinkers of the countries they represented, and the article on freedom of religious belief was thoroughly discussed.

The committee members examined ways in which human rights could be established from the broadest possible perspective, one that would include Islamic thought, Buddhist and other Asian philosophies, and Christian theology.

Former president of the Brazilian Academy of Letters Austregésilo de Athayde (1898–1993) played a major part in this process. As he would later affirm when I met him, 'Certainly such spiritual liberties as freedom of faith deserve maximum protection in modern society.'[6]

I had the privilege of publishing a dialogue (*Human Rights in the Twenty-First Century*) with Mr Athayde, who held high hopes for the twenty-first century as a century of human rights. The guarantee of freedom of religious belief and other human rights are fundamental to a democratic society.

The identification and synergistic integration of philosophical principles held by various traditions and faiths of the religious world in order to safeguard and sustain human rights – that, I believe, is an increasingly urgent challenge in the years ahead.

With regard to human rights, I'm told your father was also a pioneering advocate of the cause of gender equality and women's rights.

**Wahid:** That's correct.

In 1951, when my father was Minister of Religious Affairs, the Islamic religious teachers and judges school was the first to allow the enrolment of women. Up to that time, no one in the Indonesian congress had ever proposed or taken action in that direction. Though women could be ministers, they could not be religious teachers.

As a result of my father opening the way, there are many female religious judges today.

**Ikeda:** That's a remarkable achievement.

I've learned that at the time the Indonesian constitution was drafted, your father was a young man, having just turned thirty, but he was already recognized not only as an outstanding Islamic leader but also a dynamic, youthful political figure shouldering Indonesia into the future.

Like your grandfather, he was an avid learner who dedicated himself to attaining a well-rounded education. He taught himself English and Dutch while acquiring a broad range of knowledge and insights by reading many newspapers and journals. Through the school he founded, he introduced innovative educational reforms and actively sought to incorporate subjects other than religion into its curriculum.

The fact that he did not remain confined to the realm of religion but extended his activities to include education is a sign of his remarkable vision.

**Wahid:** In those days, the main texts in schools were Arabic religious texts, but my father sought to combine traditional Islamic studies with modern education.

When he married, I have heard, he taught his wife – my mother – to read Latin and Dutch. That's how passionate he was about education.

I was born, the eldest son, in August 1940.

My father named me Abdurrahman ad-Dakhil. Abdurrahman means 'compassionate servant' and ad-Dakhil means 'victor'.

As a matter of fact, the name derives from Abd al-Rahman I (731–88), who founded the Umayyad Emirate of Córdoba (756–929). Later, from the tenth through the eleventh centuries, its successor the Umayyad Caliphate of Córdoba ruled the Iberian Peninsula, or what is now modern Spain and Portugal.

**Ikeda:** In his speech that I mentioned earlier, President Obama cited Córdoba, the capital of the Umayyad Caliphate, together with Andalucía, as cities exemplifying the tolerant attitude of Islam.

I understand followers of other faiths, including Jews and others, played an important role in both the establishment of the Umayyad Caliphate and advancement of scholarship that took place there.

**Wahid:** Yes. At the time Córdoba was a great centre of learning and culture, in particular in astronomy, chemistry, and medicine. Historical records show that many from the Christian kingdoms travelled there to study.

23

Abd al-Rahman I, known as 'the victor' (ad-Dakhil), built the foundation for the later Umayyad Caliphate.

My father wanted me to become like that great ruler, which is why he named me after him.

**Ikeda:** It is a name imbued with deep significance and lofty hopes.

Córdoba is recognized as one of the three great cities of the Middle Ages. In one of my discussions with peace scholar Majid Tehranian, he cited Córdoba as historical proof that different religions can not only exist side by side but flourish together.[7]

Like Abd al-Rahman I, you have spared no effort to develop Indonesian society and the strong spirit of acceptance and tolerance that runs through it.

You have without a doubt lived up to the expectations that your father had when he named you after such an auspicious individual.

**Wahid:** Thank you for your kind words. I am deeply appreciative of my father's sentiments.

Compared to the name Abd al-Rahman, however, the name ad-Dakhil is not so well known in Indonesia.

That is why I later changed my name.

In the Arab tradition, sons often take their father's name.

My father, for instance, incorporated part of his father's name, Hasyim Asy'ari, into his own name, Abdul Wahid Hasyim.

I then took part of my father's name, changing mine to Abdurrahman Wahid.

Most Indonesians, however, know me by my nickname, Gus Dur.

'Dur' is a shortened form of 'Abdurrahman'. 'Gus' is a title used to refer to the son of an Islamic teacher (kiai) and has a meaning somewhat like 'elder brother'.

My father was commonly known as Gus Wahid to those who knew him well.

**Ikeda:** The narrative of your names is an apt symbol of the spirit of public service and, in return, the respect and admiration of your people, that has been handed down from your grandfather to your father, and, finally, to you, President Wahid. I find that very moving.

In Japan it is also often said that names depict the essential spirit of things. In other words, names are not just convenient labels but actually reveal a person's true nature and character.

Nichiren wrote: 'The name will invariably invoke all the blessings of the thing itself.'[8]

My mentor in life Josei Toda (1900–58), the second president of Soka Gakkai, used the name Jogai Toda as a young man. This was a pseudonym that he created for himself, meaning 'outside the castle'. He adopted it to express his resolve to protect Tsunesaburo Makiguchi (1871–1944), his teacher and first president of Soka Gakkai, standing guard, as it were, 'outside the castle' as his faithful disciple.

Mr Toda was imprisoned by Japan's militarist authorities, and while incarcerated had an enlightenment experience, in which he awakened to the ultimate principle of the universe. To reflect that, after he was released from prison he changed his name to 'Josei,' meaning enlightened.

As Toda's disciple, I had the pseudonym 'Daijo', meaning 'great castle'. This is a word that appears in the Lotus Sutra.

Toda often stressed the need to build a bastion of capable individuals, for capable individuals are the true 'great castles' of peace and culture.

At about the same time that Abd al-Rahman was establishing his emirate, a Buddhist teacher in Japan named Dengyo (767–822) was propagating the Lotus Sutra, which became the spiritual foundation of the flourishing culture of the Heian period.

In his examination of what was truly precious for a nation, Dengyo observed: 'What is a treasure? A mind that seeks the way is a treasure; those who possess this seeking mind are the treasure of the nation.'[9]

Those who dedicate themselves to the pursuit of the ennobling philosophy of humanism are able to guide history toward peace, justice, and prosperity. Such people are true national treasures.

And in that sense, it is clear that your grandfather, your father, and you are all 'treasures of the nation'.

And that leads me to ask: what were some of the childhood memories of your father that you cherish in particular?

**Wahid:** As the president of the Nahdlatul Ulama and, from Indonesia's independence, a minister of the state with important official responsibilities, my father was an extremely busy man.

Even so, I recall that he made time to play soccer with me in our garden.

I was a mischievous child, and I fell from a tree and broke my arm twice. In spite of that, my father was always very patient with me.

Our house was also crammed full with books.

As you mentioned earlier, this was because my father had a powerful interest in keeping up with world events, by reading books and journals in Dutch and English.

Having grown up in that kind of environment, I was familiar with books from a young age and read many of the world's literary classics.

**Ikeda:** It must have been a beautiful father-and-son relationship.

Encountering good books when you are young is a treasure that lasts a lifetime. It helps lay a strong foundation for life. It also has the power to foster magnanimity and tolerance. The great classics of literature are the shared spiritual heritage of humankind.

Your father naturally created such an environment for you.

I have also made an effort to familiarize my children with good books, in a natural, informal way.

I removed the doors from our bookcases at home, so that it was easy to pick a book up and browse through it. And I also told them, 'I don't have room for all my books, so I'm going to leave some of them here in your room,' placing them within easy reach under the guise of asking a favour.

Whenever I could find time from my hectic schedule, I would take them to the bookstore and tell them they could each choose three books that they fancied. I have also presented them with works that I found especially moving in my youth.

You evidently became an avid reader under the influence of your father. What works did you particularly like?

**Wahid:** I have read a great many literary classics, so that's a hard question to answer.

But if I were to mention the books that had the greatest influence on me as a youth, I would have to say *Night Flight* (1932) by Antoine de Saint-Exupéry (1900–44), *The Old Man and the Sea* (1952) by Ernest Hemingway (1899–1961), and *The Red Pony* (1937) by John Steinbeck (1902–68).

*Night Flight*, written at a time when aviation was far, far less advanced than it is today, was very compelling, with its descriptions of those early pioneers of the skies.

In those days, long-distance flights were still tremendously risky. They were a matter of life or death, and truly remarkable experiences.

That tension made for a story that is as thrilling as it is fascinating.

The words appearing at the end of *Night Flight* remain deeply etched in my heart: 'A victory weakens one nation, defeat arouses another.'[10]

I read that book when I was quite young, but it's one I would recommend to many young people today.

**Ikeda:** It's one of my favourites as well.

Johann Wolfgang von Goethe (1749–1832) was one of my beloved authors when I was a youth. In a letter Goethe wrote as a young man he records a passage from the Qur'an: 'Moses said, "Lord, lift up my heart . . ."' (Qur'an [20]:25).[11] That made a deep impression on me.

We can feel Goethe's youthful spirit from that passage as he trawled the riches of the world's wisdom and strove to forge and strengthen his own spiritual fortitude and further ennoble himself.

What are some of the other unforgettable memories you have of your father?

**Wahid:** Once when I was five years old, at about eight at night someone knocked at the door of our house.

When I opened the door, there was a man I had never seen before, quite thin, wearing blue clothing.

'Is your father at home?' he asked. 'Tell him that Hussein from Banten is here.'

When I told my father, who was resting, he immediately got up and told me to tell my mother that we had a visitor. I had never seen the man before, but my father had a very serious expression, which surprised me. I wondered what his connection to this person was, and sometime later he told me that he was just an old friend.

It was only many years later, when I had grown up, that I learned that 'Hussein from Banten' was actually the communist leader Tan Malaka (1896–1949).

He was passing incognito because he had been living in exile for many years, and was in a difficult political position, so he wanted to make sure that people didn't know of his meeting with my father.

But, as this example shows, my father always valued friendship, with little concern for a person's position or rank.

**Ikeda:** What a telling episode of your father's character and magnanimity.

**Wahid:** I also remember being taken by my father, when I was a boy, to the home of Ignatius Joseph Kasimo Hendrowahyono, chairman of the advisory board of the Catholic Party.

My father took a small packet out of his pocket and handed it to Kasimo. I wondered what was in it, so on the way back, I asked my father.

He said to me: 'Kasimo is collecting money so that Prawoto Mangku-sasmito of the Masyumi Party can buy a house. I wanted to help.'

I was deeply moved by this. The Masyumi Party sought an Islamic state, and Prawoto was its leader.

In spite of their differing views, Kasimo and Prawoto were good friends and were deeply associated as fellow Indonesians. And my father was willing to help his friends.

My feelings at that time remain deeply rooted in my heart to this day.

**Ikeda:** I am impressed by your father's loyalty to his friends.

Friendship is indeed proud proof of our humanity.

Saint-Exupéry, whose books you love, also prized friendship and sought human solidarity.

Among his writings we find statements such as: 'We discover that we are of the same fellowship. Our consciousness grows in the recognition of other consciousnesses'[12] and 'To be a man . . . is to be proud of a victory won by our comrades.'[13]

He also described the human being as 'Man, the universal yardstick of peoples and of races . . .'[14] And he argued, 'In him is the essence of my culture. In him is the keystone of my Community. In him is the principle of my victory.'[15]

Human beings can reach across all barriers and differences to form bonds of solidarity.

In 1974, at the height of the Cold War, I visited first China and then the former Soviet Union.

I was widely reproached for this decision, people asking why a religious leader would visit countries that reject religion.

But my answer was simple: 'Because there are people there. I am going to meet my fellow human beings.'

At Moscow State University, where I was invited to speak, I stated my resolve to cherish that which shines within each of us regardless of what social or political barriers may exist, just as the light shining from people's homes in the Siberian winter exudes a human warmth that can touch the hearts of those who see it.

**Wahid:** I fully understand your sentiment.

**Ikeda:** It was with that belief that in 1968, at a time when many still regarded China as an enemy state, I proposed the normalization of diplomatic relations between Japan and China.

My words stirred up a storm of criticism. I received threatening letters and telephone calls on a daily basis for some time.

But my conviction remained unshaken that it was crucial for China and Japan, as neighbours, to establish amicable relations for the sake of the stability of Asia and world peace, and for future generations.

I learned later that Zhou Enlai (1898–1976), the first Premier of the People's Republic of China, had taken note of my proposal.

In 1972, diplomatic ties between China and Japan were normalized at last.

At the Bandung Conference (Asian–African Conference), Premier Zhou said: 'We believe that if we, together with all the peace-loving countries and peoples of the world, are determined to preserve peace, peace can be preserved.'[16]

Peace and friendship must be a common effort in which every country takes the necessary steps to advance, and a process engaged by international society as a whole.

**Wahid:** I too was met with much opposition when, shortly after I became Indonesia's president, I announced a policy to establish commercial relations with Israel, with which Indonesia had no official diplomatic relations.

Fully aware of the criticism I would face, I have visited Israel several times.

To me it seems that our nation – which, for many years, has had ties with such nations as the Soviet Union and the People's Republic of China, with their policies of atheism – should make the effort to find ways to establish relations with other nations, no matter what has occurred in the past or how problematic it might be.

**Ikeda:** I agree.

In 2007, I met with Mikhail Mihailovich Bely, the Russian ambassador to Japan. Before his posting to Japan, Ambassador Bely was the ambassador to Indonesia.

Ambassador Bely prized the long-honoured relationship between Russia and Indonesia, and was delighted at the advances that had been made in various areas as a result.

He also spoke of his profound respect for you, President Wahid, and your efforts to engage in dialogue with people of different cultures and races.

Ambassador Bely noted that there are some 20 million followers of Islam in Russia, where they live and work in peace alongside the followers of other religions. It was precisely because Russia is a society comprising different religions that coexist in harmony, he explained, that his country places such a premium on intercultural and interfaith dialogue.

Dialogue among religions and cultures starts from dialogue between individuals and further blossoms through friendship.

**Wahid:** I agree.

In fact, though of course I recognize the fact that Japan invaded and occupied our country, I don't have a negative attitude toward Japan. Obviously, not all Indonesians share my feelings, and everyone has their own experiences and opinions.

My father was a friend of a Japanese merchant in Surabaya named Mr Kono.

There are good and bad people in every country. I am sure that not all Japanese agreed with the war-mongering military government that ruled Japan at that time. After all, Japanese citizens such as Soka Gakkai's first president Tsunesaburo Makiguchi and second president Josei Toda were imprisoned for their opposition to Japan's militarist authorities.

**Ikeda:** I am grateful for your acknowledgement of the Soka Gakkai history.

What you've said reminds me of Huang Shiming, the vice-president of the China–Japan Friendship Association who was always so kind and helpful on my visits to China.

Mr Huang was born in Kobe, Japan, where he lived through the horrors of war; following his postwar repatriation to his homeland, he witnessed the devastation wrought by the Japanese military invasion of China. These experiences convinced him to promote friendship between China and Japan, to which he would dedicate the rest of his life.

I also lost a family member in the war. I share his deep conviction that we must never allow another war to occur.

Mr Huang acted as an interpreter in my meetings with Deng Xiaoping (1904–97), Premier Zhou Enlai's wife Deng Yingchao (1904–92), and numerous other Chinese officials, and he also became a close personal friend. When he interpreted, his voice resounded through the Great Hall of the People.

It was during my eighth trip to China (in 1992) that I learned Mr Huang was suffering from a serious illness.

I immediately sent him a poem with wishes for his recovery:

I pray,
I deeply pray
For the day
When I will again
See your great smile.

Two years later, Mr Huang's condition had improved to the point that he could visit Japan with his wife. I was delighted when he told me that he felt much better.

At our last meeting, he said that he treasured the poem I had given him and that he felt strength rising up from within every time he read it, always encouraging him. His beaming smile on that occasion remains forever etched on my mind.

**Wahid:** That's a very moving story. Friends encourage and support one another in times of difficulty and distress. Friendship is truly life's great treasure.

**Ikeda:** Your father, who reached out to people of so many different groups and who earned the abiding trust of so many, is a model of friendship.

Though your father had a bright future as a leader of his country, I understand that he died at a young age in an automobile accident. What a horrible tragedy. It was an event of incalculable grief, not only for your family but for your country.

**Wahid:** My father died on 18 April 1953. He was thirty-nine years old.

Many in Indonesia, regarding him as the probable successor to Sukarno, lamented his untimely death.

Our family suddenly lost its main support, and heavy responsibilities fell upon my mother, an ordinary housewife who was left with sole responsibility of caring for her six children with me, then thirteen, the eldest. Her father suggested she bring us all to live in his home in Denanyar, Jombang Province, but she turned him down.

She was determined that our father's 'legacy' – his children – should receive the best possible education, so she decided to stay in Jakarta.

As a result, my brothers and I received a quality education and were able to escape ignorance. I am deeply grateful to my mother for that.

**Ikeda:** Your mother was very courageous. It must have been an extremely difficult time for her.

After her husband's death, she kept his spirit and his vision alive by striving for the growth and development of Indonesian society.

**Wahid:** Yes. My mother, Solichah Wahid, dedicated herself to society. No matter what the circumstances, she always went out of her way to make the greatest possible positive contribution to the people.

In support of my father's dedication to the NU, she took on a central role in the women's movement for Islam, the Muslimat.

She also served as a representative in the Indonesian congress, where she won the respect of many and came to be loved as 'the mother of all in society'.

Wherever I went, people would say to me, 'You're Solichah's son, aren't you?' Everyone I met had a story to share with me about something my mother had done for them.

Naturally, their words filled me with pride as her son. I learned of my mother's kindness, warmth and strength not just from observing her in person, but from the words of the many grateful people she helped.

**Ikeda:** Both your father and mother led lives of great distinction, and their children, responding to the example set by their parents, have also become great individuals.

The achievements of your family through three generations, starting with your grandfather, are indeed immortal.

One of my friends, Arun Gandhi, is the grandson of Mahatma Gandhi and the founder of the M. K. Gandhi Institute for Nonviolence.

The Gandhi family also has a century-long tradition, spanning three generations, of fighting against racial discrimination.

I will never forget Arun Gandhi telling me that on a personal level, he has tried to gather together the light of his grandfather and use it as a guide by which to live his life and to develop himself as a human being.

He also said that his father had taught him that whenever a member of the Gandhi family encountered injustice, wherever it might be, he or she must stand up and oppose it.

My mentor Josei Toda often pointed out: 'The third generation is decisive; it is the crucial generation [of any legacy].'

As the third Soka Gakkai president, I have striven to carry forward the spirit of presidents Makiguchi and Toda, and dedicated myself to the struggle to build a robust grassroots network for peace in our world.

In that context, I find my dialogue with you, President Wahid, who have embraced and succeeded the noble spirit of your family as a member of its third generation, especially significant.

I firmly believe that as long as an organization or a country preserves and carries forward its core spirit and values, it will not lose the dynamic force that ensures future progress.

# THREE

# The Struggles of Youth and the Search for Answers

---

**Ikeda:** I would like to begin by offering my deepest condolences for the 30 September 2009 earthquake in Northern Sumatra.

Having experienced earthquakes of similar destructive power, we in Japan are only too well aware of the grief and adversity the victims must be experiencing. In addition to praying for the peaceful repose of those who died, I fervently hope that the area will recover as expeditiously as possible and the stricken will be able to return to a life of safety and normalcy as quickly as possible.

**Wahid:** Thank you for your kind words. I am deeply touched and appreciative. Our country is fully dedicated to recovery.

**Ikeda:** I am certain you must be extremely busy, but I want to thank you for taking the time to return to our dialogue.

**Wahid:** It is I who am grateful. I believe our dialogue is very important, and I look forward to its continuation.

**Ikeda:** My mentor in life, second Soka Gakkai president Josei Toda (1900–58), earnestly hoped for the peace and security of Asia and the happiness of its people. Envisioning a future of friendly relations with the countries of Asia, he often said to young people that everything starts from sincere, heart-to-heart communication. To this end, he believed it was important to discuss the tales and literature of one another's countries and promote peaceful, cultural dialogue.

This has been my conclusion, too.

Indonesia is a rich, diverse storehouse of stories and epics.

Among the great historic narratives of your country is the *Chronicle of the Kings of Pasai*.

**Wahid:** Yes. In about the thirteenth century, Pasai was the first Islamic kingdom in Indonesia. It is formally known as the Kingdom of Samudra Pasai (1267–1521).

**Ikeda:** The story begins with the discovery of a princess in a bamboo stalk, doesn't it? When the king tried to cut the stalk with a machete, a girl of extremely beautiful countenance emerged from the bamboo.

**Wahid:** Yes, that's right.

The king named the girl 'Putri Betung' (Bamboo Princess), and he and his queen lovingly raised her.

**Ikeda:** The story of the Bamboo Princess has been shown to be quite similar to *Taketori Monogatari* (The Tale of the Bamboo Cutter), a Japanese tale from a thousand years ago.[1]

In that tale, one day an old man finds a bamboo tree with a light emanating from its root. As he approaches the light, he discovers a lovely baby girl, whom he takes home to be raised by him and his wife. Her beauty is unmatched by anything in this world, so they call her 'Kaguya-hime' (Shining Princess). Many young scions of the nobility seek her hand in marriage, but she refuses them all. Then one day a messenger arrives from her home, a city on the moon, to bring her back. Though she regrets having to part with the parents who raised her, Kaguya-hime returns to the moon.

When Japanese learn of the story of your Bamboo Princess, they immediately think of it as the Indonesian version of Kaguya-hime, and are not only surprised by the similarities between the two tales, but also look to Indonesia with a greater sense of familiarity and enchantment.

**Wahid:** Yes, they are quite similar. That's extremely interesting. It's delightful to discover the common humanity that all cultures share.

35

**Ikeda:** Our two cultures have many other similar narratives and tales. Research has shown that Indonesia is an important source of much of Japan's folklore.

Traditional tales help convey the gentle, unspoiled landscape of a culture.

What do you see as the 'landscape' of Indonesia's soul? In particular, I'd be interested in hearing about the place you grew up.

**Wahid:** I was born and raised in a typical Indonesian farming village, and I have fond memories of its sights and sounds.

I came into this world on 4 April 1940, in the village of Denanyar, in Jombang Province, East Java. About half the population of the village were farmers, earning their living by tilling the land.

**Ikeda:** Historian Arnold J. Toynbee was moved by the scenery of your beautiful farming villages, writing in a book describing his travels: '[N]ow I find myself once more in a world in which Man coaxes Nature with inexhaustible love and labour.'[2] And: 'I feast my eyes on those tiers of rice-trays, with the hurrying clouds reflected in their still waters. This ancient land is oozing with water and teeming with life.'[3]

Such descriptions bring to mind scenes in which nature and human beings are both aglow with life.

Incidentally, what kind of games did you play as a boy?

**Wahid:** As a child, I enjoyed swimming in the river that ran in front of the local *pesantren* (Islamic boarding school). After classes, I immediately went for a swim with my swimming buddies.

On the south side of the village was a hill called Tunggurono, meaning 'Forest Guardian'. That was another place I played.

During the Majapahit Empire, the royal princes viewed the approaching enemy forces from Madin and Kediri from this hilltop.

I also enjoyed playing *obak* (hide-and-seek), and following the rail trucks that carried the sugar cane to the sugar processing factory. There were many sugar cane fields in the area.

**Ikeda:** I see that you were able to grow up in a happy and carefree manner, immersed in the beauty of nature and farmland bounty.

Speaking of carts, there is a famous story by the Japanese author Ryunosuke Akutagawa (1892–1927) in which he beautifully describes his fascination with a rail truck, his joy at taking a riding in it, and his simultaneous anxiety at being carried too far from his home. In the old days, there were many such rail trucks in Japan. What were you like as a boy?

**Wahid:** I was quite scrappy. When my friends said something I thought was wrong or unfair, I could get very argumentative.

I suppose it's no surprise that I remain fond of argument and I am still quick to voice my objections to anything I think is wrong, even to this day.

**Ikeda:** I see. But that's the proper way to behave. It's important to speak up and say what needs to be said, no matter to whom you're speaking. That's the special privilege of youth, and the way to forge strongly held convictions.

When I founded the Soka schools I made one of the guiding principles for students there: 'Express your convictions in a forthright manner and uphold justice with courage.'

The Soka schools, with that motto as a guideline, now field one of the top debate teams in Japan.

**Wahid:** That's wonderful.

**Ikeda:** Speaking of an argument, I am reminded of my first meeting with then Soviet president Mikhail Gorbachev at the Kremlin (in July 1990).

Japanese–Soviet relations were tense at the time, and it was uncertain whether President Gorbachev would be making an official visit to Japan.

I opened our meeting by saying: 'I have come here to argue with you, President Gorbachev. Let's talk freely, and let the sparks fly, for the sake of humanity and for Soviet–Japanese relations!'

President Gorbachev seemed a little startled, but he was quick to understand my intent and, with a warm smile, replied that he, too, enjoyed honest, open dialogue. It was during our meeting that day that he expressed his intention of being the first serving Soviet leader to visit Japan.

Our friendship has prevailed through the turbulent currents of the times, grown ever deeper over the years, and we have even published a dialogue together.

I hope to engage in some lively discussions with you, too, President Wahid, in the course of our discourse.

**Wahid:** I believe that people need to keep discussing until they have fully understood one another. That's what makes you the best possible dialogue partner for me.

You were born in 1928. Do you remember your childhood very well?

**Ikeda:** For generations, our family business was to grow and produce *nori* (edible seaweed).

Everywhere you looked, bamboo poles for growing the *nori* were set in the seabed at regular intervals, stretching from the shallow waters off the shore out into the bay.

Salty breezes from the ocean danced and tittered across the open fields along the coast, which bloomed with a riot of fragrant flowers throughout the seasons. I may have lived in the city, but such scenes were more reminiscent of the countryside.

My favourite place to play as a child was on the beach, with glittering waves of gold and silver lapping at the sands. During the New Year's holiday, we would fly kites there, losing track of time in our frolic.

My elementary school was surrounded by farm fields. When the water of the rice fields froze in the winter, we used to break bamboo stems in half and strap them to our feet as skates.

Winter was the peak season for harvesting *nori*. We would get into our skiff and go out before dawn into the cold winter wind, sticking our hands into the freezing water to collect the *nori* from the bamboo poles. I often got up early with my parents and helped them.

Though the work was hard and we were busy, my mother was always bright and cheerful.

Though modest, my own experience has enabled me to empathize with those who engage in agriculture and fishery and the manifold difficulties they face. You won't be able to endure the rigours of farming and fishing if you aren't as patient and persevering as you are hard working.

But demanding as it is, working together with nature in order to provide sustenance for our lives is equally joyous and fulfilling.

You also witnessed the arduous labours of farmers from the time you were a child. It must have been a major factor in enriching your own life as well.

**Wahid:** Agriculture and generally living in a way that respects and treasures nature's blessings is a tradition that for the majority of Indonesians is deeply rooted in their daily existence.

In Indonesia today approximately half the population is engaged in farming or fishing.

**Ikeda:** From ancient times, Japan has been the recipient of many agricultural boons from Indonesia.

The potato, which some suggest was introduced to Japan by way of Indonesia in the seventeenth century, saved the lives of many Japanese who were faced with famine or starvation. Indeed, the Japanese word for potato, *jagaimo,* is evidently derived from 'Jakarta tuber', in homage to Indonesia.

According to genetic research published in 2008, the staple strain of rice grown in Japan, Japonica, developed from rice grown in such countries as Indonesia.

From ancient times, agricultural exchange has transcended national and cultural boundaries. Agriculture is the most sublime of occupations as it produces the food that sustains our lives.

**Wahid:** I agree completely.

**Ikeda:** The Buddhist teacher Nichiren wrote: 'A king sees his people as his parents, and the people see their food as Heaven.'[4] In writing this, Nichiren makes clear that the people are the essence of a nation, and the food that sustains our lives should be included among the most treasured of all bounties.

Agriculture is also the mother of culture and the wellspring of the wisdom with which we may live in harmony with nature.

A society that fails to accord agriculture its due respect, then, will eventually fail to value life, degenerating into barbarity and suffering widespread stagnation. This, I believe, is a spiral in which such societies inevitably plummet.

In addition, farming villages keep alive the precious heritage of traditional culture that tends to be lost in cities.

**Wahid:** Exactly. When I was a boy, study of the Qur'an was the centre of village cultural life, and that study produced many individuals of strong faith. That culture persists today.

In my hometown, there was also a Chinese cemetery, known as the Bong Cino. I often went to play there with friends.

There was also a place for cultivating the traditional Javanese spiritual practice known as *kejawen*, and it still exists.

**Ikeda:** Your hometown was a place in which many peoples, religions, and cultures, coexisted and mingled.

What were some of the time-honoured tales and theatrical dramas that you were familiar with?

**Wahid:** One form of traditional culture of which I was very fond from childhood was *wayang kulit*, the shadow puppet performance.

Some of the characters appearing in the plays are from the Hindu culture, which I also respect. The fictional characters of the plays serve an important role as models for behaviour in daily life.

**Ikeda:** I'm told *wayang kulit* has a history of a thousand years and is one of the representative traditional dramatic arts of your country.

The *wayang* combines such ancient Indian epics as the *Ramayana* and the *Mahabharata*, religious ideals of Hinduism, Islam, and Buddhism, and ancient Javanese culture. It is fascinating for its rich subject matter, narratives, and expressive language. It is indeed symbolic of Indonesia.

Did any particular *wayang* story make a special impression on you in your boyhood?

**Wahid:** I was especially influenced by the character Kumbhakarna, the younger brother of King Ravana in the *wayang* stories.[5] He was a warrior who often engaged in religious fasts and served as a state minister.

In the epic, as he prepares for the final battle, Kumbhakarna meets the virtuous Sugriwa and says to him: 'I will follow your commands and, as proof of my love of the people and the kingdom, I will protect the kingdom of Alengka Diraja. To do so I will don a robe expressing my dedication to my people and my kingdom. I will demonstrate my loyalty, if necessary, with my death.'

This is the *wayang kulit* version of the story, and marks the depths of Kumbhakarna's commitment to his people and kingdom.

**Ikeda:** You have followed this same path marking the essence of leadership since your own youth.

To devote one's life to the struggle to serve one's people, and the courage, dedication, and compassion it entails – that is the mark of a great leader. In this, you stand as an example for all to emulate.

**Wahid:** Thank you.

Looking back on my life, I was only five years old when World War II ended.

The war was only a very small part of my life. In that regard, my life has been like those of most children born after it.

As a child I lived in a farming village, and we had no information about people who lived outside our community. Though I was born during the war, I didn't have a full, personal understanding of its cruelty.

Your childhood, President Ikeda, was spent in the midst of the period in which the turmoil of the Great Depression spread throughout the world, which then pressed onward into the darkness of World War II.

You must have very special feelings about having lived under a militarist regime.

Would you be willing, for the sake of the young people of Indonesia, to share some experiences of the war that you witnessed in your youth?

**Ikeda:** War is terribly cruel.

In my family, my four older brothers were all drafted, one after another. My eldest brother Kiichi, who I respected deeply, died in the fighting in Burma – present day Myanmar – at the age of twenty-nine. Our family was only informed of his death nearly two years after the war's end. To this day I remember the sight of my mother, who was always so strong, her back shaking with grief as she wept upon learning the news.

Once, when my brother had returned from the war in China on redeployment leave, he angrily confided to me: 'The Japanese army is too cruel for words. With what we're doing to the Chinese, I can't help but pity them.' These were, in a way, his parting words to me.

**Wahid:** I have heard of the deep love you had for your mother and eldest brother.

**Ikeda:** During the war, a young American soldier parachuted out of his plane, which had been shot down by Japanese soldiers. He landed near the place where we were residing at the time. The airman was beaten with sticks and kicked by an angry mob until the military came, blindfolded him, and led him away.

When I told my mother about this, she said: 'How terrible! The poor boy! His mother must be so worried about him.'

So many young people lost their lives in the war. And so many mothers shed tears of grief as a result. That is why I am absolutely opposed to war.

**Wahid:** Thank you for those invaluable accounts.

Those who devote themselves to peace and the welfare of others usually have some formative or galvanizing experience that is the foundation for their strong convictions.

The power of your message for peace is the result of your continuous struggle for peace that arose from your glimpses of the true nature of war when you were a boy.

**Ikeda:** As I once discussed with the late Dr Joseph Rotblat (1908–2005), who served as secretary general of the Pugwash Conferences on Science and World Affairs, war transforms human beings into beasts. It is an act of madness that can drive even those who loathe barbarity to barbarity.

As the great Indonesian writer Sutan Takdir Alisjahbana (1908–94) warned, the lesson of war is that even a person with a conscience, once he forgets he has one, can expose his innate brutality.[6]

It was from my anger at and resolve to overcome the diabolical nature of war, which makes us lose sight of the worth and dignity of human life, that I wrote in the opening of my life's work, the novel *The Human Revolution*: 'Nothing is more barbarous than war. Nothing is more cruel.'[7]

Moreover, as the opening to *The New Human Revolution*, the sequel to that novel, I penned the words: 'Nothing is more precious than peace. Nothing brings more happiness. Peace is the most basic starting point for the advancement of humankind.'[8]

**Wahid:** Those are indeed deeply moving words.

War exposes the ugliest aspects of human beings. And that is true not only of wars waged with other countries. There are many cases in which, though people are closely related, they are placed in a situation resembling war by power and political struggles.

I personally resent or hate no one and have tried to build good relations with all. Even so, I was at risk of losing my life on three occasions, for political reasons. And those who tried to kill me were people with whom I had good personal ties. That is why I understand only too well your statement that war and conflict can transform people into barbarians.

As a result of having been involved in such conflicts, I have been and continue to this day to be the target of many forms of criticism and abuse.

But I am proud of the fact that I continue to fight for the sake of the people, and I have confidence in the truth of my convictions, so I can endure anything. I have come to think of it all as a personal test.

**Ikeda:** History shows us that all great thinkers and reformers have been criticized and persecuted.

Mahatma Gandhi (1869–1948), the champion of nonviolence, took a far-sighted view of worthy movements, observing that those that change the world pass through several phases in public reaction, starting with indifference and moving on through scorn, criticism, and oppression before they finally come to be respected.

Similarly, I am certain that your principled actions, President Wahid, will earn the acknowledgement, appreciation, and acclamation that you rightfully deserve for building the foundation for Indonesia's advance.

I believe that your message of tolerance and peaceful coexistence, which you have imparted not just to Indonesia but throughout Islamic society and the world, will shine ever brighter over time.

Did your family have a considerable influence on the strong convictions you hold?

**Wahid:** Yes. I inherited some of them from my grandfather, and many from my father as well. For me, this is a source of great pride.

When I was a boy, I often slept beside my grandfather. He would lie down next to me and talk to me about many things as I drifted off to sleep.

One of the lessons he certainly taught me was the spirit of tolerance and acceptance, of respect for all other people.

I am very fortunate to have had such a fine model and great educator so close to me in my life.

**Ikeda:** That's a very important point.

I would say that a person who spends his formative years among people he can respect, people whose integrity he can observe close at hand, has a very blessed childhood. And when that person embraces the lessons imparted during that period in life and remains true to them over a lifetime, that person can be said to have lived a life of great distinction.

Adolfo Pérez Esquivel, the Argentinian champion of human rights with whom I engaged in a dialogue, is one such individual. Though experiencing much hardship in her life, his grandmother had faithfully dedicated herself to the service of others. Dr Esquivel proudly refers to her as his hero.

The family is the first and finest school.

I still remember the lessons my parents taught me as a child, such as to be considerate and always tell the truth.

And I still vividly recall the acts of kindness by others when I was young.

For example, during World War II, I had contracted tuberculosis, and even though I occasionally coughed up blood, I was forced to work in a military stores factory, which only exacerbated my condition.

An elderly nurse working in the factory's first-aid room was very kind to me, even taking me to a hospital where I could be examined by a proper doctor. With a compassionate smile, she sought to buoy my spirits by saying, 'You're too young to give up. You've got to make it through this.' I remain grateful to her to this day.

The more depressing and desperate the state of society, the more brightly shines the spirit of good-hearted ordinary men and women who empathize with the plight of others and offer them sincere encouragement.

**Wahid:** I also learned a great deal from those who have supported me in my life. Not just my grandfather and father, but my teachers and people in my community taught me the importance of behaving with sincerity and integrity to all and cultivating a spirit of tolerance and acceptance.

I respect those who never give up, no matter what hardship comes their way. There are people who, even in a situation when one feels the urge to run away, are able to rouse not only themselves but also many others. I look to you, President Ikeda, as such an individual.

**Ikeda:** You are too generous.

**Wahid:** You are a person of true integrity, and you are always true to your word.

At the Peace Art Festival held in Jakarta in July 2008, attended by many top Indonesian government figures and guests from various fields, I said to the more than 4,000 assembled participants that you and SGI (Soka Gakkai International) have engaged in and put into practice numerous reforms in religious life and humanism.

I have always been deeply impressed by those who, like Mahatma Gandhi, love peace. You are one such person.

**Ikeda:** Thank you again for your kind words.

It is you, President Wahid, who has distinguished yourself in the service of peace, humanity, and democracy. I have spoken of this to Japanese youth on many occasions.

Your words will surely be a source of encouragement to our SGI members in 192 countries and territories around the world.

They are striving tirelessly to contribute to the peace and prosperity of their respective societies as outstanding citizens and community members.

The Peace Art Festival also commemorated the fiftieth anniversary of diplomatic relations between Indonesia and Japan.

It was jointly sponsored by the Indonesian Muslim Artists and Culturalists Institute (LESBUMI), which is part of the Nahdlatul Ulama (NU); the largest youth organization in your country, the Indonesian Youth Congress (KNPI); and the SGI.

I would like to take this opportunity to thank you for all the help and support we received on that occasion, from you and everyone else.

**Wahid:** The pleasure was all ours. The friendship of the SGI is extremely important both to me and to Indonesia. The SGI remains true to the path of goodness that it confidently teaches and practises. This is something that we need to learn from them.

For many years I have been the leader of the NU, the largest Islamic organization in our country.

I have constantly striven to remain absolutely true to the founding ideals of the NU, which was established by my grandfather.

The duty of both the NU and myself personally is to firmly uphold the ideals of the founder.

As a matter of fact, LESBUMI, the cultural organization that assisted with the Peace Art Festival, faced the prospect of disbandment in the past. At that time, we were able to revive it by steadfastly upholding the spirit of the founder.

You have been active as the leader of the SGI for many years, President Ikeda. Can you tell me about your initial encounter with second Soka Gakkai president Josei Toda?

**Ikeda:** I first met Josei Toda on 14 August 1947. The meeting occurred exactly two years after Japan's capitulation in World War II.

The military regime had made State Shinto the nation's spiritual pillar to rally support for the war, but when Japan was defeated, that pillar had been shattered and lost.

The sudden and drastic change in our value system left us youth uncertain about what to believe in, and we suffered from a sense of spiritual emptiness, doubt, and confusion.

As people struggled to recover from the difficulties brought on by our nation's defeat, they looked deep within themselves for the true path of life, a strong spiritual pillar in which they could believe. I was one such young person.

Nothing is more worthy and precious than life. Having painfully come to that realization, I greedily devoured the great works of world philosophy and literature and, participating in reading groups with friends, spent my days on an intellectual and spiritual quest.

It was at that time that a friend invited me to a discussion on a philosophy of life and took me to a Soka Gakkai meeting. It was there that I encountered Mr Toda for the first time.

Wishing to candidly present matters that were troubling me, I asked Mr Toda three questions: How can we live a good life? What is true patriotism? What do you think of the Japanese emperor?

Mr Toda answered all three without any hesitation or obfuscation, and with directness, clarity, and sincerity. What most impressed me was learning that he had been imprisoned during the war for his opposition to the militarist authorities and had remained true to his beliefs during the two years of his incarceration. In my heart, I knew that this was a person I could trust.

I didn't fully understand Buddhism at that time, but I was drawn to Mr Toda as a person and to his sheer force of character, and that is what made me decide to join him on the same path of religious faith and practice.

**Wahid:** You were impressed not simply by Mr Toda's words but by his unflagging faith throughout his struggle in prison and his behaviour as a human being.

**Ikeda:** Yes, precisely.

Nichiren wrote: 'The purpose of the appearance in this world of Shakyamuni Buddha, the lord of teachings, lies in his behaviour as a human being.'[9]

The fundamental purpose of religion is to polish and perfect our character. The true worth of religion shines in our actions.

A short time after that initial encounter with Mr Toda, he gave me a job at a publishing company he ran, employing me as the editor-in-chief of a boys' magazine.

Motivated by the wish to offer inspiring dreams to our readers, I was in charge of every facet of the magazine, from planning, editing and writing to commissioning articles and illustrations, which I personally retrieved; I was also responsible for the magazine's layout and proofreading. In the process I met many famous writers.

But in the economic turmoil of the early postwar years, Toda's businesses fell on difficult times and he was forced to stop publication of the magazine. He then began a credit association, but that also faltered and ultimately failed, forcing him to the brink of bankruptcy.

Most of his employees deserted him, cursing him as they left, but I alone remained at his side, supporting him both personally and professionally, taking the full brunt of all his business difficulties as I struggled to protect him from his creditors and detractors.

At that time I sent him a poem I had composed:

As I serve my mentor of an old, mystic bond,
Unchanged will I myself remain, though others may change.

I have never forgotten Toda's smile when he read it.

**Wahid:** Your ties to your mentor Mr Toda supported and sustained you through a youth of suffering.

**Ikeda:** Yes, that's correct. I no longer had time for the night school I was attending, so Mr Toda, an outstanding educator, offered me private instruction in a wide variety of subjects. He taught me political science, economics, law, philosophy, history, chemistry, physics, astronomy, and so forth, covering every subject and the full range of world thought and literature for about ten years, up to his death.

This study at what I call 'Toda University' became my irreplaceable spiritual foundation.

My mentor's peace philosophy is distilled in his statement that he wanted to rid the world of misery.

He also advocated the idea of the global human family, a concept consonant with the contemporary idea of global citizenship, and issued a declaration calling for the abolition of nuclear weapons, making his foremost legacy to youth the creation of a world without war or nuclear arms. In the more than half-century since his death, I have striven continuously to make my mentor's vision and ideas a reality.

**Wahid:** I am deeply moved by the noble spirit of mentor and disciple that you describe.

Contemporary society has countless problems it must surmount, but it is very rare to meet a leader who embodies such true beliefs in his life.

I don't think it was a mere accident that you encountered Mr Toda in your youth, filled with hardship.

The fact that you have inherited and kept his teachings alive to the present day is proof of that.

I also look up to my grandfather and father as my mentors in life and have dedicated my existence to seeing that their ideals are realized in the present.

With the spirit of my grandfather and father, who dedicated themselves to the growth of Indonesia, clasped firmly in my heart, at a recent seminar held at the National Islamic University, I lectured on the development of democracy in Indonesia.

In my lecture I urged students not to become corrupt leaders and to lead lives of goodness.

**Ikeda:** That is a message that I would definitely like to communicate to the youth of Japan and the world.

There is a Javanese saying that admonishes, *Ojo dumeh*, or 'Do not become intoxicated by power.' Power is indeed a toxic elixir that can bring about one's undoing.

In the same vein, Mr Toda used to call on young people to maintain a strict vigil over politicians.

To protect democracy, it is imperative for citizens, with young people in the lead, to become wise and keep a close watch on government.

It is my fervent hope that political leaders of honesty and integrity, working for the happiness of the people above all other considerations, will emerge in a steady stream from the younger generation.

**Wahid:** Yes, I agree completely.

Fighting for the welfare of society as a whole and the happiness of the people has also been my deepest conviction.

As a religious person, I have upheld a commitment to an open-hearted, accepting attitude toward others, to living an honest life, and to the welfare of society as a whole and the happiness of the people being the foremost priority, to be secured at all costs.

**Ikeda:** In this confused and troubled twenty-first century, those are all important guidelines for those of us with deep religious convictions.

The renowned Indonesian poet and dramatist W. S. Rendra (1935–2009), who passed away in August 2009, stressed the importance of a highly developed moral self.

Rendra recited one of his poems at a culture festival held by SGI-Indonesia in 2002, attended the World Boys and Girls Art Exhibition we organized, and supported and encouraged our activities in many ways.

I was told that after viewing the World Boys and Girls Art Exhibition he had described the 'prayer' for a better world underpinning the children's works as being both wonderful and deeply moving. For children, the poet said, the world is an unsullied, open society. Violence must not be tolerated in the world, he asserted, and adopting the proper morals is essential to establishing peace. He also said that he thought the exhibition should be held nationwide.

**Wahid:** Rendra was a national poet, known to every Indonesian. His statement that violence must not be tolerated in the world, and that adopting the proper morals is an essential condition for peace is, in my opinion, a perfect embodiment of his beliefs.

**Ikeda:** Adults are the cause of war and violence. And countless innocent children are the victims.

Children are born to achieve happiness. They are entitled to learn and to develop their potential to the fullest in a world of peace.

49

Children are still untainted by prejudice. Their minds are unfettered and shine with abundant creativity.

The spirit of global citizens inherently dwells within them.

It was with this conviction that I originally proposed the SGI-organized World Boys and Girls Art Exhibition, which began in 1988, just before the end of the Cold War.

Supported by the United Nations Educational, Scientific and Cultural Organization (UNESCO), the exhibition has displayed representative works collected from more than 100 countries at venues around the world and has been very well received.

Found in every painting is a message for peace, brimming with the children's dreams, hopes, and courage. Those created by Indonesian children, showing boys and girls living in harmony with nature and animals, are also featured. Young viewers in Japan, having discovered so many different places and people portrayed in the works, have seen their dreams and worldviews blossom.

I believe that this heart-to-heart communication and inspiration fosters open minds; it is the seed that will grow to flower as a century of peace filled with the happy laughter of children.

To nurture the hearts and minds of children is to nurture the future.

We adults need to think seriously and act wisely to see what we can do to make that happen.

# FOUR

# Toward a Century of Human Rights

---

**Ikeda:** A life dedicated to pioneering a new age is one of untold toil, buffeted by storms of adversity. Yet the dedication to that effort shines with powerful conviction that is unclouded by doubt.

Raden Ajeng Kartini (1879–1904), a pioneering advocate of women's liberation in Indonesia, wrote: 'There must be someone who sets the example'[1] and 'if one has but the courage to begin, many will follow her.'[2]

Your wife Shinta Nuriyah Wahid (b. 1948) is a true pioneer and model for the rights and improved status of women and has been active in this cause for many years. She was previously a journalist for the magazine *Zaman* ('Era') and with a friend, a scholar, has authored a book on improving the social status of Muslim women.

**Wahid:** Yes. Thank you for mentioning my wife's accomplishments.

She has made important contributions to local society, focusing in particular on activities for women.

She is the founder of PUAN Amal Hayati, a *pesantren* (Islamic boarding school) for young women, and in addition has engaged in activities for women's rights.

I have the highest esteem for my wife's activities to ensure that women enjoy equal rights to men in their lives.

For that reason, I am planning on co-authoring a book with her.

**Ikeda:** That's wonderful.

51

In addition to your wife's activities for women's rights, I was deeply impressed by the fact that she remains undeterred by being confined to a wheelchair because of a traffic accident in 1993. She has gone on to earn a master's degree in women's studies from the University of Indonesia.

She has said: 'I believe one must constantly learn. If one loses the will to study, one falls behind.'[3]

I would like to share her words with as many women and young people as possible.

Her life of conviction stands as a shining example in this century in which women will emerge truly triumphant, inspiring hope in millions and warranting the highest praise.

**Wahid:** Thank you very much for your warm words. I would like to express my appreciation in my wife's stead.

We have been married almost forty years and my wife has always worked hard for our family's happiness, in addition to her numerous social activities.

Since my daily round of activities is also quite busy, to be honest we have had little time to sit down together and talk at length.

Nevertheless, I think we have a deep mutual understanding. I am sure you agree with me about this, President Ikeda, but I believe this is very important.

**Ikeda:** Yes, you bring up a vital point.

Understanding and trust are crucial in a marriage. This is something that my wife and I can empathize fully with.

No one knows better than my wife the reality of my struggle to embody the spirit of my mentor, second Soka Gakkai President Josei Toda. And likewise, I believe I know my wife's sincerity and steadfast spirit better than anyone else.

The bond of husband and wife can only deepen over the years should they share a commitment to help others and better society as long as they live.

Nichiren wrote: 'A man is like the wings of a bird, a woman like the body. If the wings and the body become separated, then how can the bird fly?'[4]

Husbands and wives are truly soulmates engaged in a shared struggle, then, ennobling one another as they take flight together in fulfilling the grand purpose of their lives.

I understand that many of our women readers are interested in hearing some of your recollections of the time when you and your wife were first married.

**Wahid:** Certainly.

We were married in mid-1968. As a girl, my wife graduated from a *pesantren* and then went on to study at the State Institute of Islamic Studies (Institut Agama Islam Negeri) in Yogyakarta. She wanted to study Islamic law *(syariah)*, but traditionally that area of learning was not open to women.

But when my father was Minister of Religion, for the first time all fields of study were opened to women, who were allowed to study on an equal footing with male students. As a result, my wife was a member of the most advanced group of female students in Indonesia.

When she entered the State Institute of Islamic Studies, her parents decided that it would be best if she and I were officially married before she began her life as a student in Yogyakarta.

There was, however, an impediment to our marriage.

**Ikeda:** As one of the country's founders, your father played a major role in advancing women's rights. It was through his wise actions, then, that your wife was able to study the subject of her choice.

It's my understanding that Islam fundamentally favours both men and women to acquire learning.

What stood in the way of your marriage?

**Wahid:** Simply put, I wasn't in Indonesia.

As I mentioned earlier, from the age of twenty-three I was studying in the Middle East, and in 1968 I had moved from Egypt to Iraq, where I was studying at the University of Baghdad.

In Islam, the marriage ceremony is a mutual pledge of faithfulness, the *akad nikah.*

I was still living as a student at the University of Baghdad, and I didn't have time to return home for the ceremony. After discussions between the two families, we found a solution.

It was a rather radical solution, so I'm sure those who attended the ceremony must have been surprised.

An eighty-one-year-old man walked up and stood at the side of the bride.

53

He was my maternal grandfather, KH Bisri Syansuri (1886–1980). He acted as my surrogate, making our wedding possible.

Later, when I had returned to Indonesia, my wife and I were able to celebrate the occasion together, in person at a wedding reception we held in 1971.

Do you have any special memories about your wedding, President Ikeda?

**Ikeda:** Your story reflects the dedication with which you and your wife concentrated on your studies in your youth for the sake of your country's future.

My wife and I were married the year after my mentor Josei Toda had been inaugurated as second president of Soka Gakkai, a time when I had managed to restore his business fortunes after a hard-fought struggle into which I devoted my entire being.

Aware of our feelings for one another, Mr Toda acted on our behalf and set out alone to visit both sets of parents and receive their permission for the marriage.

I wasn't present, but apparently he had the temerity to ask my father, whom he had never met until then, 'Will you entrust your son to me?' After thinking it over for a while, my father replied that he would.

Then Toda said that he had a fine marriage proposal. My father replied, 'I have entrusted my son to you so you may do as you please.'

Toda set our wedding date on the auspicious day of 3 May 1952, exactly one year to the day after his inauguration as Soka Gakkai's second president.

It was a very simple ceremony with only the closest relatives, and Toda's speech was both brief and heartwarming: 'Men must have strength. The kind of man who makes his wife and children worry cannot do great work in society.' And he concluded, 'The two of you have pledged yourselves to your faith at a young age, and I hope you will continue to adhere to your faith for as long as you live.'

**Wahid:** Your wedding was a shining ceremony reflecting the bonds of mentor and disciple.

My wife and I don't have great wealth to leave to our children, but we are proud of our long and happy marriage.

In it, we have fostered our children's abilities to take an active part in society, and their capacities to do their best in their chosen fields of endeavour. This is our legacy to them.

**Ikeda:** That is indeed the greatest treasure that any parents can bequeath to their children.

Providing one's children with material security is important, but more than that, a central responsibility of parents is to teach them the riches that lie in the depths of their lives. That, I believe, is what it truly means to educate a person as a human being.

People inherently possess an immense capacity for goodness – the compassion to care for others, the yearning to make a positive contribution to society, the wisdom to perceive the truth, the courage to right wrongs, the inner fortitude and tenacity to endure life's tribulations, the creativity to learn from adversity. Life itself is, indeed, the greatest treasure of all.

Nichiren taught: 'Life is the most precious of all treasures. Even one extra day of life is worth more than ten million *ryo* of gold.'[5]

I believe summoning forth the goodness inherent in our lives – in other words, fostering morality – is the fundamental mission of both education and religion.

Recently in Japan a documentary about a young Indonesian man has captivated its audience, moving many viewers.

The film chronicles the life of Endang Arifin, who died while trying to save a drowning junior high school student at a beach in Miyazaki Prefecture in the summer of 2007.

He was in Japan as a fishery trainee and, while at the beach on his day off, he heard a girl cry for help; he and his friend dived into the water to save her. While other swimmers managed to save her, as Endang was swimming out toward her he was swept away by a powerful current and drowned.

The film portrays the gentle, pure spirit of the young man and expresses the grief of those who knew him.

Titled *Mas Endang*, the documentary has been shown at forty venues in both Indonesia and Japan.

**Wahid:** The *mas* in the title of the documentary is a respectful form of address for a young man in Indonesian. The title alone expresses a feeling of deep affection.

The film has been introduced on television and other media in Indonesia.

I would like to express my most heartfelt gratitude to the people of Japan, who have so kindly commemorated this Indonesian youth whose life was cut off in its prime.

**Ikeda:** Though he wasn't a strong swimmer, Endang jumped into the ocean without a moment's hesitation as soon as he heard the cry for help.

I have heard that his father, when informed of his son's death, said that his son must have reacted that way because he had always taught him to help those who were in distress.

I pray from my heart for his peaceful repose. People in Japan have taken his noble spirit to heart. He will not be forgotten.

This reminds me of an episode from a report that was presented to the United Nations General Assembly in November 2001.

Entitled 'Crossing the Divide: Dialogue among Civilizations', the report was drafted by a Group of Eminent Persons commissioned by then Secretary-General Kofi Annan.

The report relates the story of two families, unknown to one another, on summer vacation at a beach in the Middle East. The child of one of the families swimming in the water seemed about to drown. The father of the other family saw this and jumped into the water, returning the child to safety, but he himself was drowned before he could reach the shore. The family of the rescued child was Jewish, and the father who rescued the child was Muslim. Ignoring all such distinctions, the man risked his life to save the drowning child.

The report was published immediately after the September 11, 2001 terrorist attacks in the United States, which only made it more meaningful and reaffirmed the importance of building a society that transcends all divides.

**Wahid:** That's very true.

As I said previously, I learned the importance of peaceful coexistence and the spirit of tolerance from my grandfather and father, and have carried them forward as my own deeply held beliefs.

The Simon Wiesenthal Center has honoured me for my work for human rights. I believe they did this because of my efforts to protect minority rights.

No matter how earnestly we call on people to choose peace over hatred, people cannot change their lives if they are not free.

Unfortunately, many in Indonesia do not really understand the significance of this award from the Center, but I want to stress the absolute indispensability of protecting and respecting the rights of minorities.

Even if my activities are met with opposition, I have the right to my opinions, and I think people should recognize that the reasons that I must engage in my activities are clearly present in our society.

**Ikeda:** As you say, the question of how we may best protect the rights of minorities is one that the entire world seeks to answer.

I have visited the Simon Wiesenthal Center in Los Angeles twice.

In June 1996, I gave a lecture there on the life and legacy of the first president of Soka Gakkai, Tsunesaburo Makiguchi, who opposed the Japanese militarist authorities during World War II and died in prison for his beliefs.

In my lecture, I spoke about Mr Makiguchi's principles and actions, based on his conviction that rebuking and removing evil is inseparable from embracing and safeguarding good, and that we should not be content with passive goodness – we need to become a person of courage and mettle who can actively strive for good.

I stressed that true tolerance is one and the same with the refusal to accept any form of violence or injustice that threatens the worth and dignity of human life, and is exemplified by a life in which we do not ignore the plight of others but traverse upon the path to happiness together.

You are famous, President Wahid, for embodying this spirit of true tolerance and actively reaching out to engage interfaith dialogue.

In June 2007, in fact, the Wahid Institute partnered with the Simon Wiesenthal Center's Museum of Tolerance to hold a multifaith gathering against violence on the theme of 'Tolerance Between Religions' in Bali.

**Wahid:** Yes, representatives of Islam and Judaism, as well as Christianity, Hinduism, and Buddhism participated in the conference.

The director of the Institute of Oriental Philosophy, which you founded, also took part.

The conference issued a joint declaration pledging to respect religious diversity and calling for an end to acts of violence and retribution. I cannot help but believe that religious leaders have an ever-growing mission to promote world peace and the happiness of humanity.

In relation to this, I'd like to mention a political leader that I have respected from my childhood: King Airlangga (991–1049), who allowed the Buddhist state of Medang (Mataram) to flourish in Java.

King Airlangga believed that religious diversity is important within a culture, which is why all religions in Indonesia refer to him with the respectful title *Mpu*, meaning 'teacher'.

My emphasis on the importance of religious diversity is rooted in the tradition established by King Airlangga.

**Ikeda:** Airlangga possessed outstanding leadership abilities, and in addition to religion he marshalled the strengths of his people in such realms as agriculture, trade, and the arts. He is widely acknowledged as a wise sovereign who led his kingdom to prosperity in a short span of time.

His life was filled with dramatic vicissitudes.

In the midst of his wedding ceremony at age sixteen, an enemy kingdom attacked the palace, and he was forced to flee deep into the forest. But it is said that the three years he spent in the forest had forged the young king's mettle.

Eventually, at the urgent plea from his people, he vowed to restore the kingdom and rose up with adamantine resolve.

After building up his forces, he made his move. Devoting himself to improving both domestic governance and foreign relations, he ultimately succeeded in reestablishing the kingdom. It was a dramatic comeback victory that had cost the king over twenty years of trial and toil.

Once the realm was firmly established Airlangga abdicated to lead the life of a Buddhist hermit, dividing his kingdom into two to prevent his sons from warring over its succession, with each enthroned in his own new realm.

He tempered tribulation into resilience in his youth; he possessed the fortitude to rebound from adversity; he demonstrated tenacity and industry over a period of many years; and he made judicious decisions regarding his succession. Airlangga was indeed a brilliant ruler, with many lessons to teach us – including the importance of prevailing in the end, no matter what obstacles we face along the way.

Learning from the great leaders of history when one is young becomes a priceless asset that endures for a lifetime.

You have also been active for many years as a journalist, which I understand was your dream since childhood.

**Wahid:** Yes, I have continuously contributed editorials to newspapers and magazines as a public voice. In my youth I actually had three dreams.

One was to be a pilot, the other to be a physician, and the third to be a newspaper columnist. The only one I succeeded in realizing was the third.

I began writing editorials for the Indonesian magazine *Tempo* and the newspaper *Kompas* in the early 1970s. I was in my thirties then, and I had a regular column dealing with social problems.

Through that column, I had a platform to discuss the events taking place in contemporary society at large, outside the realm of the usual issues relating to religion, and in my columns I consistently stressed the need for pluralism, religious tolerance, and the protection of minority rights.

While calling for reform within the realm of Indonesian Islam, I also played the role of a bridge between the government and the *umat* [community], to prevent conflicts between the two.

Today I publish a weekly column in *Seputar Indonesia*.

I am happy that my column is popular and many readers seem to enjoy it.

**Ikeda:** Your writings are a treasure not only for Indonesia but for Asia and the world.

Speaking from personal experience, writing is a rigorous struggle.

**Wahid:** I know that you have enjoyed a very long writing career and even now continue to compose a serialized novel.

**Ikeda:** From the time I was a boy it was always my dream to someday compose a work that would move people's hearts.

My life's work, the novel *The Human Revolution*, was published serially starting on 1 January 1965. That was seven years after my mentor's death.

I began writing the work – a record of my mentor who stood alone amid the ruins of postwar Japan and established a Buddhist movement with the aim to ameliorate suffering and bring peace and prosperity to society – because I felt it was my duty as his disciple.

Over twelve volumes I depicted the latter half of his life, from his emergence from prison to his achievement of the tremendous growth of Soka Gakkai.

When I had finished composing the last line I wrote these final words before setting down my pen:

Volume 12 of *The Human Revolution* completed on 24 November 1992.
Dedicated to my late mentor, Josei Toda. By his disciple, Daisaku Ikeda.

Then, starting in 1993, on 6 August – the date of the atomic bombing of Hiroshima – I began the novel's sequel, *The New Human Revolution*, which I continue to write today.

I have halted composition briefly from time to time to collect and collate reference materials, but I have been writing the two novels now for nearly forty-five years, and have reached more than 5,700 serial instalments. *The New Human Revolution* is said to have set a record in Japan for being the longest serialized novel.

Once newspaper serialization begins, no matter how demanding your schedule or your physical condition, you are always facing deadlines that will not wait.

On many occasions I began writing my day's portion of the novel late at night, only after returning home from a very busy day's work.

I recall how in the midst of my gruelling schedule, attending functions and travelling to encourage my fellow Soka Gakkai members throughout Japan and around the world, I was too pressed to put pen to paper and was forced to dictate the instalment and send a tape to my office in Tokyo.

On other occasions I was so exhausted by my duties that I didn't have the strength to even pick up a pen, so I dictated instalments to my wife, which I duly noted in the margins before handing it in to my editors.

What do you bear in mind when writing your editorials and columns?

**Wahid:** When I write editorials, there are no particular restrictions. My consistent aim, however, has been to oppose forces that are oppressing the people.

**Ikeda:** That's an admirable stand.

The modern history of Indonesia shines with individuals, starting with you, President Wahid, who have fought bravely against injustice.

As the Indonesian journalist and author Mochtar Lubis (1922–2004) so stirringly wrote, we must protect the people and 'we must have the courage to pledge our whole beings, our physical and spiritual selves, to the fight for the common people.'[6]

**Wahid:** Mochtar Lubis was famous in Indonesia for his intrepid struggle for truth.

**Ikeda:** In his treatise, 'On Establishing the Correct Teaching for the Peace of the Land', Nichiren embodied that spirit as well. Compelled by an earnest wish to relieve the onerous suffering of the Japanese people and committed to voicing the justness of his cause, he wrote: 'I cannot keep silent on this matter.'[7] His commitment to truth is also foundational to our activities to advance the cause of truth and justice.

In the same work, asserting that peace is the true foundation for the security and happiness of ordinary people, Nichiren also wrote: 'If you care anything about your personal security, you should first of all pray for order and tranquility throughout the four quarters of the land, should you not?'[8]

In a survey by a national Japanese newspaper on works deemed relevant to the twenty-first century, 'On Establishing the Correct Teaching for the Peace of the Land' came in second.[9]

Out of his concern for peace and the happiness of the Japanese people, Nichiren denounced the errors of the first full-fledged military regime to rule Japan, the Kamakura Shogunate (1192–1333). This resulted in him being persecuted repeatedly for offences he did not commit, placing his life at serious risk.

In spite of government oppression, however, he courageously wrote, in a declaration of spiritual freedom: 'Even if it seems that, because I was born in the ruler's domain, I follow him in my actions, I will never follow him in my heart.'[10]

Those words were included in *Birthright of Man: An Anthology of Texts on Human Rights*, prepared under the direction of Swiss philosopher Jeanne Hersch and published by the United Nations Educational, Scientific and Cultural Organization (UNESCO) to commemorate the twentieth anniversary of the Universal Declaration of Human Rights.

The Buddhism of Nichiren is the Buddhism of the people. He reached out to and taught the common people, inspiring his peers with immeasurable courage and hope. His letters, written in an accessible vernacular writing form rather than in the classical Chinese used by many Buddhist teachers of the day, are precious texts of spiritual guidance.

Through his words and deeds, Nichiren strove for the happiness of the people; he stood together with them and worked to empower them to the very end. His life and legacy would later influence the educator and thinker Shoin Yoshida (1830–59), underpinning the latter's belief that ordinary people must become the primary drivers of historical change. Yoshida's message was carried on by his disciple Shinsaku Takasugi (1839–67) and others, helping to impel the Meiji Restoration.

**Wahid:** I see. I have always had a strong interest in Japanese history, particularly the Meiji Restoration, so I find what you've said highly instructive.

The process by which the Meiji Restoration came about, with many cumulative events eventually leading up to such a grand transformation, is indeed fascinating.

**Ikeda:** That is an insightful observation.

The activities of Soka Gakkai, based on Nichiren Buddhism, have led to the revitalization of the oppressed and disadvantaged, serving as a major source of their empowerment.

In the organization's early days it was often ridiculed as a gathering of the poor and sick.

But my mentor Mr Toda remained entirely unfazed by this mean-spirited public reception and declared: 'It is the mission of a genuine religion to save the poor and the sick. Soka Gakkai is the ally of the common people.

'When Soka Gakkai is derided as nothing more than a gathering of the poor and sick, our retort is: "Well, just how many of the poor and sick have you helped, then?"' These words of my mentor will always remain the pride and covenant of Soka Gakkai.

**Wahid:** The Nahdlatul Ulama (NU) also continues to strive for the happiness and welfare of Indonesian society, based on the teachings of Islam.

At present we have a special focus on education, and we support the activities of 200,000 *pesantren* schools throughout Indonesia. In addition, while engaging in *Dakwah Islamiyah* (Islamic propagation efforts), we are striving to promote friendship based on solidarity, transcending differences; we are supporting education in accord with Islamic values, fostering pious and pure-hearted followers of Islam with broad learning; in the social and cultural realms, we are striving for the people's welfare and culture in accord with Islamic and humanitarian values; we emphasize the economic welfare of the people and engage in efforts to ensure that the benefits of development are fairly distributed. In addition, we support other activities and projects that have broad social benefits.

**Ikeda:** I can see that the NU is active not only in the field of religion but in many diverse areas.

The *raison d'être* of religion is to provide such wide-ranging contributions to society. Together with its sectarian purpose, a religion also has a humanitarian and social mission to carry out.

Professor Tu Weiming of Harvard University, with whom I engaged in a dialogue, stressed this point.

He said: 'I take some satisfaction in noting that, although secularization is often designated as a defining characteristic of modernization, religions continue to have a presence in the modern world.'[11]

And speaking of the role of religious leaders, he added: 'Religious leaders are certainly responsible for the well-being of their faith communities. In the face of the new demands of the global situation, however, they are called upon to assume the role of public intellectuals as well.'[12] And: 'As such, they are obligated to respond to issues beyond the immediate concerns of their communities.'[13]

President Wahid, you are not only a distinguished religious leader but are also fulfilling your role as a public intellectual in a remarkable manner.

**Wahid:** Thank you for your kind words. Dr Tu's words are right on the mark.

There is much dissatisfaction and unrest in our world today. Not only do we face the political issue that true democracy is not being realized, but many decry the problems of the economy and environment.

Young people, driven by a desire to find quick answers to these problems, are being drawn to and falling under the influence of radical and fundamentalist groups. But I believe that the vast majority of young people in Indonesia are pure and warm-hearted and have strong consciences.

That is why I wish to say to young people, with all my heart, 'Open your heart and act with honesty.'

I want to open the way so that each and every young person can advance straight ahead, without confusion, along the correct path for the twenty-first century.

To that end, I am determined to keep speaking out against all forms of social iniquity and injustice.

# FIVE

# Cultural Exchange is the Source of Creativity

---

**Ikeda:** In October 2009, we welcomed a delegation from the University of Indonesia to Soka University.

The University of Indonesia is one of the foremost institutions of higher learning in South-East Asia, with a history of 160 years. It has trained the leaders of your nation's independence and been instrumental in Indonesia's subsequent development; it has a reputation for fostering individuals of both learning and the highest moral character.

On his visit to our university, Rector Gumilar Rusliwa Somantri said that young people around the world today share the same problems, as well as the responsibility to resolve them. This is a pivotal age, he continued, in which each individual needs to strive to build a civilization for all humanity, transcending race, national borders, and all other divides, and establish a world in peace.[1]

It is with the deepest gratitude that I note that twenty years have gone by since the University of Indonesia and Soka University concluded an exchange agreement, and the number of exchange students between the institutions is on the rise.

As Soka University's founder, nothing would please me more than to see the young people of Indonesia and Japan work together in common cause to advance the noble mission of creating a civilization of humanity and global peace.

**Wahid:** I have heard that the University of Indonesia recently conferred an Honorary Degree of Philosophy and Peace on you.

I would like to sincerely congratulate you on the receipt of this honorary doctorate, presented to you by our oldest and most eminent university.

As I mentioned previously, my wife is a graduate student at the University of Indonesia, and many of my relatives are graduates.

**Ikeda:** Thank you. I am indeed honoured and humbled to have received the award.

**Wahid:** I clearly remember my visit to Soka University. It made a deep impression on me. While many universities today have become commercialized, Soka University does not place priority on money, income, and increasing its profitability.

It has a very well-funded scholarship programme for students who cannot afford the tuition, and I know that it keeps the tuition at a relatively low level.

As this indicates, I hope that Soka University will continue to practise this commitment to the humanitarianism that the university upholds as its ideal.

**Ikeda:** Thank you for your warm words of support.

We at Soka University were extremely honoured and delighted to be able to present you, President Wahid, with an honorary doctorate in 2002. Your visit to our university was a very meaningful event for us. Please allow me to express my gratitude once again.

Our times demand further educational and academic exchange.

Among the graduates of the University of Indonesia with whom we have engaged in such exchange is Dr Fuad Hassan (1929–2007), Indonesian Minister of Education and Culture. Dr Hassan has said: 'Peacebuilding should be our common goal through genuine intercultural dialogues, free from prejudices and stereotypes.'[2] And: 'Cultural diversity as a permanent feature of human society should eventually evolve as a phenomenon of creative diversity.'[3]

A peaceful world will not be a homogeneous one, nor one of differences in conflict with one another. It will be a world in which multiple elements inspire one another to create a higher, diversified creativity.

The first decade of the twenty-first century will soon reach its close.

The question before us is whether we can set forth toward the creation of a century of peace and harmonious coexistence, with the lessons of the twentieth century, an age of war and violence, firmly in mind.

The year 2010, when we embark on that new decade, is critical.

I hope to identify and pursue a path that will unfailingly bring about such a transformation together with you, President Wahid, whose insights on humanity and tolerance are without peer, as well as with other luminaries of your country.

**Wahid:** I, too, am earnestly engaged in this endeavour.

**Ikeda:** The world today faces towering challenges on a planetary scale, from the unprecedented global economic crisis to climate change and the proliferation of nuclear weapons.

None of these daunting issues can be resolved by any single nation alone, requiring resolution by the entire global community.

Given our predicament, the G20 Summits in response to the recent economic crises have newly evolved into important, regularly scheduled forums for promoting international economic cooperation. And Indonesia, I understand, is a member of the G20.

**Wahid:** Yes, that's right.

Up to now, global economic problems have largely been discussed at the G8 gatherings, but with the recent economic crises, that group has been expanded to the G20.

Along with this expansion, the Asian nations of China, India, South Korea, and our country of Indonesia have been added to the discussion.

From the Islamic world, in addition to Indonesia, the Kingdom of Saudi Arabia and the Republic of Turkey have been included.

**Ikeda:** Indonesia's role, as a nation that is both Asian and Islamic – two key factors in envisioning the world of the twenty-first century – is certain to continue to grow.

Since the end of the previous century, I have called for the need to expand participation in such global summits of the world's leaders and progressively revise them into a 'Summit of Responsible States'.

This is based on my belief that the only way to resolve global issues is to find ways to share responsibility on a global scale, a process that requires engaging in the exchange of a wide range of viewpoints and reaching consensus and agreement based on dialogue on an incremental basis.

US President Barack Obama, who has played a pivotal role in establishing the G20 gatherings as routinely held sessions, has said: 'We can no longer meet the challenges of the twenty-first-century economy with twentieth-century approaches. And that's why the G20 will take the lead in building a new approach to cooperation.'[4]

As if to presage the present global economic meltdown, Japan experienced a similar crisis when its bubble economy burst in 1990. Putting the lessons that Japan has learned from that experience to use, our country needs to work together with the rest of the world's nations to overcome the present crisis. To do so, new structures for international cooperation are indispensable.

**Wahid:** Indonesia wishes to do everything possible for that purpose as well.

I have long believed in the need for Indonesia to play a major role in international society.

For many years, protection of territorial integrity has been the priority in Indonesian foreign relations.

Those problems have now been resolved, and the time has arrived when we need to redirect our diplomatic priorities to responding to the problems of the global age.

In other words, our focus needs to be on the welfare of the world as a whole, on the welfare of humanity as a whole.

**Ikeda:** That is a very important statement.

And you have personally acted as a pioneer in blazing that path.

As you say, every nation must proactively engage in actions taken for the sake of the world and humankind, marshalling their respective abilities and resources into one united effort. We simply do not have a choice any more. It is no exaggeration to say that the fate of this century rests on our success in accomplishing that.

In the twentieth century, after two world wars, the world was polarized into two opposing blocs during the Cold War. Yet, just when we thought that the Cold War had ended, the world was struck by the tidal forces of globalization, resulting in a growing new hegemony led by the United States.

Now, triggered by the world financial crisis that started in the US, the world is developing into a multipolarity.

Will this engender peace and harmonious coexistence based on respect for diversity and plurality? Or will it encourage each nation and territory to turn inward, intensifying tensions and conflict? The world, I believe, stands at a major crossroads.

In this regard, I think it is vital that we exercise the utmost wisdom to reflect deeply upon the history of exchange among civilizations, studying and learning from the past.

Which is why I would like to turn back the clock of history to examine the propagation of Buddhism and Islam in South-East Asia, and how they coexisted in harmony there.

**Wahid:** A noteworthy moment in the history of the transmission of Buddhism was its introduction to Indonesia by the Chinese monk Faxian (*c.337–c.422*) in the early fifth century.

The historical sources tell us that on his way back to China from India, Faxian landed on the coast of Java.

**Ikeda:** Aware that the Buddhist canon in China remained incomplete, Faxian set out on his journey because he had wanted to introduce the so-called 'Three Baskets' – the sutras, treatises, and discipline texts – that had not yet been transmitted to his homeland from India. He was some sixty years old, a very advanced age at the time.

Departing from Chang'an in China in 399, he crossed the treacherous Taklamakan Desert, scaled the towering Pamir Mountains, crossed the Indus River, and finally, after a journey of six years, reached India.

He spent nearly another six years in India and Sri Lanka, where he devoted his time to studying Buddhist life and discipline texts while assembling precious Buddhist scriptures. He chose to return to China by sea, passing through Indonesia. A powerful windstorm would send his ship off course to Qingzhou (present-day Shandong Province) before he finally arrived back in China. By that time he was in his seventies.

But he immediately set to work translating and introducing the texts he carried back from India, numbering six works and sixty-three volumes. He also composed a chronicle of his travels, *A Record of Buddhistic Kingdoms*.

In the afterword to that work he wrote:

Looking back on what I have gone through, involuntarily my heart throbs and a perspiration breaks out. That, in the dangers I encountered on foot or otherwise, I did not spare this body, is because I devoted my energies wholly to this one object; therefore I risked my life in places where there was no certainty of escape, in order to accomplish even a fraction of what I hoped for.[5]

It is a timeless testament to Faxian and his indomitable resolve in prevailing over every conceivable geographical obstacle at his advanced age.

**Wahid:** It is truly astonishing that he accomplished what he did at his age. But it was through his arduous efforts that the spirit of Buddhism was introduced to Indonesia.

Further study of the actual exchange taking place in the region from India to China at that time will certainly have important lessons for us today.

**Ikeda:** I agree.

In his travels from China to India and back, Faxian passed through more than twenty kingdoms. Of course it was extremely arduous in terms of the geography he had to surmount, but never in his travels was he caught up in a war. This is a striking fact to me.

It suggests that in the vast region of Asia at that time, exchanges among cultures and individuals were taking place peacefully.

In the region from India to Central Asia, in particular, Buddhism had spread widely and was firmly entrenched in most of the kingdoms. Peaceful relations also seem to have existed between kingdoms.

Today, while we have overcome the logistical obstacles that Faxian faced with advances in modern transportation systems, the challenge of expanding avenues of spiritual and cultural exchange have become greater than ever.

One of the Buddhist texts translated by Faxian depicts Shakyamuni teaching Buddhism until the very end, just before his death.

It describes how the people of a market town Shakyamuni visited in India were of different skin colours, and wore diverse styles of clothing and accoutrements. Observing this, Shakyamuni is recorded as telling his followers to regard the town's inhabitants as the same as the many brightly hued deities in the heavens.[6]

In this we see the spirit of tolerance and acceptance in Buddhism, which regards the differences among races, peoples, and cultures as the embodiment of the great diversity of life.

**Wahid:** Buddhists made an important contribution to Indonesia as a multi-ethnic nation.

Faxian was an individual of great learning, and his knowledge and the spirit of Buddhism was inherited by the Indonesian Buddhist kingdom of Srivijaya.

Three spiritual legacies from that period have been faithfully handed down through the ages to present-day Indonesia: respect for teachers, dedication to the public good, and building a good relationship with society.

**Ikeda:** Indeed. All of those elements are core ideals in Buddhism.

The Tang-dynasty (618–907) Chinese Buddhist monk I-Ching (635–713), writing in *A Record of the Buddhist Religion as Practised in India and the Malay Archipelago* – which he composed during the time he resided in the Srivijaya kingdom – repeatedly stresses that '[I]n the fundamental principles of the Law of the Buddha, teaching and instruction [to respect one's teachers] are regarded as the first and foremost.'[7]

Writing of the two individuals who trained him, with the strictness of a caring father and the compassion of a loving mother, I-Ching wrote:

> The two teachers were to me as sun and moon giving light. Their virtues may be compared to those of the Yin and Yang (i.e. 'the positive and negative principles that pervade nature'). The point of my sword of wisdom was sharpened by them. And by them also my body of the Law was nourished. They were never tired in their personal instruction.[8]

Writing in Indonesia, I-Ching left a record revealing the way of a disciple – to reply to the debt of gratitude owed to one's mentor by blossoming as an individual – that transcends time and national borders.

Nichiren's Buddhism also underscores the importance of this debt of gratitude. It teaches a way of life that fully appreciates one's parents, teachers, society, and all living beings, repaying all those who have contributed to one's existence.

*A Record of the Buddhist Religion as Practised in India and the Malay Archipelago* not only depicted the actual lives of Buddhists in South-East Asia in great detail, but is also an important historical resource describing local societies and customs at the time, isn't it?

**Wahid:** Yes, it is. I-Ching, who visited the Srivijaya kingdom in the latter part of the seventh century, after Faxian's time, notes through his personal experience of living in the kingdom the many different cultures existing in his era. He also wrote of an expedition from Pekalongan to the depths of central Java that occurred as part of the territorial expansion of the Srivijaya kingdom.

On that occasion, the people of the Srivijaya kingdom encountered the Kalinga Empire, in the present-day Wonosobo Regency, whose people practised Hinduism.

But the Srivijaya leaders, without forcing the local people to convert to Buddhism, later proceeded south to what is now Yogyakarta.

In the second half of the eighth century, another Buddhist kingdom, the Sailendra dynasty, flourished in central Java. This was the dynasty that built Borobudur in Magelang, near Muntilan.

**Ikeda:** Borobudur is a famous Mahayana Buddhist temple, registered as a World Heritage Site by UNESCO. It stands among the largest Buddhist monuments in the world, the foundation of its pyramid structure 120 metres on a side, the entire structure more than thirty metres high.

**Wahid:** Yes, it is one of the Seven Wonders of the World. One unique feature of Borobudur is that it is entirely made of stone, with no cement or mortar holding the stone blocks together.

**Ikeda:** It is indeed an architectural wonder.

The walls of its corridors are carved with reliefs depicting the life of Shakyamuni and episodes from the scriptures. I have heard that there are 1,460 reliefs in all.

They are of the highest artistic quality. The French painter Paul Gauguin (1848–1903) collected photographs of Borobudur and, carefully studying its beautiful depictions of the human form, often applied them in his work.

Indonesian culture has travelled many routes to inspire the world.

Arnold J. Toynbee (1889–1975) described the emotions that swept through him when finally visiting Borobudur in this way:

> Before I pore over them I must mount to the summit and view the whole monument as the architect meant it to be viewed, with the green lawns at its foot, the forest-clad mountain for a drop scene at the back, and the

glassy rice-fields embroidering the fertile plain to the east. Wild Nature; Nature tamed by Man; the genius of the architect and the sculptor; the earthly life of the comprehensive poem about the mystery of the Universe, a symphony of the inaudible music of the spheres.[9]

Religious feelings and emotions fire our powers of creativity and imagination, from which poetry, painting, and music spawn. They inspire us to engage in some form of expression.

The blossoming of the creative powers of humanity is the wellspring of culture and testament of genuine peace.

**Wahid:** That is a lovely way of putting it.

As a proud part of the cultural heritage of Indonesia, Borobudur is visited by many Muslims as well as Buddhists.

As you have noted, each stone of the monument's many corridors is carved with images. I see this as a symbol of the spirit of peace and indomitable energy of the people of those times.

Similar to the history of the transmission of Buddhism to Indonesia, the transmission of Islam to our country was also conducted peacefully.

Generally, Islam and its related culture is thought to have been introduced in about the seventh century, at the time of the Buddhist kingdom of Srivijaya. At the time, Srivijaya was flourishing as a maritime realm controlling the trade routes of western Indonesia, including the Strait of Malacca. As a result, it was visited by many Arabian, Persian, and Indian merchants.

Islam and Islamic culture were brought to Indonesia by such individuals. As these merchants and seamen carried goods to Indonesia, they also introduced Islamic morals and values. Through interaction with these Islamic traders, Islam began to spread among Indonesian merchants.

From its beginnings, Islam has never had a special class of missionaries.

In other words, the transmission of the teachings of Islam was not the duty of a particular group, but of Islamic society as a whole.

Islam was also propagated peacefully without force or violence.

**Ikeda:** That's an important historical fact. Merchants played an especially active role in bringing Islam to Indonesia, then.

Your friend the writer Pramoedya Ananta Toer also described merchants as the most vigorous and cleverest members of the human race:

merchants are called *saudagar*, which means 'people with a thousand wiles'.[10] And:

> It's no coincidence that the Prophet, may Allah's blessing be upon him, began his career as a trader. Traders understand the realities of life. In commerce people are not concerned with people's social status. They don't care if someone is of high or low rank or even a slave.[11]

When we exhibit an open-minded spirit, liberated from the psychological barriers that cause us to discriminate against others, we find a rich and nourishing wisdom and vitality emerge from within us.

It is certainly true that historically speaking commercial activity has promoted an atmosphere of openness and brought the world closer together.

The Silk Road was also a trade route, as well as a route for the communication of culture and religion.

The land-based Silk Road linked India and China and was the route along which Buddhism was transmitted, while a trade route that can be called the 'Maritime Silk Road' served to connect Arabia and Persia to Indonesia and propagate Islam.

**Wahid:** Exactly.

The first regions to which Islam was transmitted were northern and western Sumatra and central Java.

After the decline of the Srivijaya kingdom, the Muslim population grew remarkably on Sumatra, especially in the Samudera Pasai Sultanate (1267–1521). From Samudera, Islam spread to Malacca, Minangkabau, Riau, Tapanuli, and elsewhere.

Islam was transmitted to Java during the reign of Ratu Sima (674–731).

The tradition of tolerance that characterizes the history of Indonesia can also be seen in the attitude of followers of other religions toward Islam.

The Hindu–Buddhist kingdom of Majapahit on Java allowed the propagation of Islam. With the decline of the Majapahit kingdom from about the fifteenth century, Islam spread quickly. The Wali Songo (nine sacred protectors) played a major role in spreading Islam widely throughout Java.

**Ikeda:** In propagating Islam, the Wali Songo were said to have respected traditional culture and arts, such as the gamelan orchestra and the *wayang kulit* puppet drama.

**Wahid:** Yes. One Wali Songo, Sunan Kalijaga, was known for the flexible approach he took to local culture. He and his disciples succeeded in protecting the local culture that we enjoy today.

As part of their propagation of Islam, the Wali Songo often employed songs, so that children would be able to grasp its teachings. The songs symbolized the teachings of Islam.

The *wayang kulit* that I was familiar with from childhood was created and further developed by the Wali Songo, from the style of *wayang* that existed prior to their appearance. They employed *wayang* to spread Islam.

**Ikeda:** Recently scholars in Japan have collected, translated, and published *wayang* plays deriving from the ancient Indian epic, the *Mahabharata.*

According to their research, the Wali Songo cast Prince Bima who appears in the *wayang* play *Dewa Ruci,* to represent the teachings of Islam.

In pursuit of eternal life and the Perfect Being, and in search of life's true meaning, Bima travels to unexplored mountains and the middle of the ocean, until finally he receives the teaching that the perfected life is to be sought within himself.

Birth and death are also a theme of the *wayang* plays.

Bima also appears in the *wayang* play *The Liberation of the Pandawa Brothers*, where he speaks of where we come from, who we are, and where we are to go – or life's quintessential meaning and lesson.

The painter Gauguin also titled his great work on human existence, 'Where Do We Come From? What Are We? Where Are We Going?'

While I'd like to discuss this subject later on, Buddhism was born from the search for the way to resolve the four sufferings of birth, ageing, sickness, and death.

To delve into the challenge of birth and death, from which none can escape, and the search for the timeless essence of life – these are indeed universal themes for humanity.

Incidentally, I understand some of the Wali Songo were not from Indonesia.

**Wahid:** Yes, the first, Maulana Malik Ibrahim (d. 1419), is said to have been of Persian origin.

Concerning the spread of Islam, it was next introduced to Sulawesi, but did not develop with the momentum it exhibited in Sumatra and Java, because in a struggle for political power, a non-Islamic kingdom opposed the religion.

Islam spread quickly in Kalimantan from the time of Sultan Suryanullah (1520–50).

In the end, the influence of Islam was felt throughout Indonesia, and Islamic kingdoms such as the Sultanate of Demak (1475–1548), the Kingdom of Pajang (1568–86), the Sultanate of Mataram (1588–1681), and the Sultanate of Banten (1527–1813), as well as Islamic kingdoms on Kalimantan, Sulawesi, and Sumatra, were founded.

**Ikeda:** Historically speaking, President Wahid, why do you think Islam was so widely accepted and spread so broadly throughout Indonesia?

**Wahid:** I think there were various factors involved, but the equality and tolerance taught by Islam played a major role, in my opinion.

These teachings agreed with our spiritual tradition.

Islam teaches that there are no differences of status or class among people. No one is superior or inferior, no one better or worse than anyone else. All are the servants of God, according to Islam.

The Qur'an also teaches: 'you have your religion and I have mine' (Qur'an [109]:6).[12]

The Prophet Mohammed respected differences of opinion. Because of this teaching, I have been able to exchange opinions with people of all different religious and philosophical backgrounds.

These days I often meet and discuss matters with the Confucian teacher Bingky Irawan, the head of the Indonesian Confucian Association, and Nugroho Tri Cahyadi of the Indonesian Communion of Churches in Indonesia.

**Ikeda:** I have heard that since independence Indonesia has given official recognition to various religions in addition to Islam, including Buddhism, Hinduism, Catholicism, and Protestantism. In recent years, Confucianism has also been recognized as an official religion in Indonesia.

Prior to this development, as part of your advocacy of respect for the beliefs and religions of minorities, you have consistently and actively urged official recognition of Confucianism.

Equality and tolerance are also central principles of Buddhism.

Shakyamuni Buddha declared: 'Not by birth does one become an outcast, not by birth does one become a brāhmaṇa.'[13] He also said: 'By one's action one becomes an outcast, by one's action one becomes a brāhmaṇa.'[14] In other words, one's true worth as a person is not determined by such external factors as pedigree or birth but the spirit and faith that lies within.

Nichiren Buddhism expounds a principle known as 'the cherry, the plum, the peach, the damson'.[15]

The cherry, plum, peach, and damson, while all bloom to the fullest with their own unique and distinct beauty, exist in harmony. In the same way, while all human beings are rooted to the great earth of the worth and dignity of all life and our shared humanity, they concurrently exhibit their own unique qualities in a manner unique to themselves, creating our diverse and pluralistic world.

**Wahid:** Cherry, plum, peach, and damson – that is indeed a profound teaching.

In addition to the tolerance and equality I mentioned earlier, one other vital factor, in my opinion – and this seems particularly true in the case of Indonesia – is that when Islam spread it respected the pre-existing culture and customs.

As the leader of the Nahdlatul Ulama, I have always underscored the importance of respecting traditional culture and customs, while preserving the essence of the teachings of Islam as our foundation.

In our *pesantren*, too, I have stressed the need to not only nurture *ulama* (Islamic scholars and leaders) but also expand our perspective to include fostering those who embody religious values rooted in the community.

**Ikeda:** Buddhism also teaches a precept known as 'following the customs of the region'.[16] According to this principle, as long as the local culture and customs do not violate the essential teachings of Buddhism, they are to be respected and preserved, and Buddhism needs to be adapted to the special characteristics of a place and the needs of the time.

The aim of Buddhism is peace and happiness for all, and a prospering society. That is the purpose of our faith and practice.

Buddhism cannot exist divorced from society or reality. That's why Buddhists must always strive to behave in a sensible, positive manner and as good citizens contribute to the welfare of others, the community, and peace. This is the underlying spirit of both Soka Gakkai and Soka Gakkai International (SGI).

In our actions firmly rooted to the community, we have consistently focused on one venue in particular – the discussion meeting. At these meetings, members, regardless of their gender, age, profession, or level of education, assemble in small groups at the local community level to share the joys and sufferings of life, study Buddhism, deepen their faith, and encourage and support one another in their growth as individuals.

**Wahid:** That is a very important endeavour. Does this tradition date back to the origins of Buddhism?

**Ikeda:** Yes, it does. Buddhism began to spread into the world from gatherings of small groups similar to our discussion meetings.

Having attained Buddhahood beneath the bodhi tree, Shakyamuni pondered over ways to communicate the content of his enlightenment to others. He finally decided to first expound his teachings not to people at random but to the five others who had long engaged in austerities with him – a scene that is depicted in a relief at Borobudur.

Nichiren Buddhism also places strong emphasis on small groups of followers who gather, learn, engage in dialogue, and encourage one another. Which is why Soka Gakkai has consistently placed great emphasis on discussion meetings.

On one occasion first Soka Gakkai president Tsunesaburo Makiguchi fielded a question from a young man who suggested that it might be more effective to hold large, lecture-style meetings, to present Soka Gakkai's message to greater numbers of people. Mr Makiguchi's response was clear. 'I don't think that's true,' he said. 'The only way to communicate with others about life's problems is through dialogue. A lecture can never be personal or immediate for its listeners.'

In the years leading up to World War II, Makiguchi continued to hold discussion meetings, sharing the humanistic Buddhism of Nichiren with others and imparting courage and hope to them, even while being subjected to surveillance by the infamous Special Higher Police and its efforts to undermine his work.

Soka Gakkai has inherited Makiguchi's convictions and carries them on to this day. As has the SGI. Through discussion meetings held in 192 countries and territories around the world, our membership has grown on a modest but steady basis as people take part in a circle of dialogue in which they can speak frankly and truly communicate with one another.

Informed people around the world who have participated in our discussion groups have expressed their admiration for the way we work.

Many of them have particularly credited discussion meetings as serving as a basis for developing democracy.

I believe democracy begins when people come together and mutually affirm one another's worth and respect as fellow human beings. Indeed, many thoughtful individuals have observed that the discussion meeting, where people of every walk of life gather to share their joys, sorrows, and friendship, is a distillation of democratic ideals.

**Wahid:** I believe it is paramount for people to affirm one another's humanity.

Through the process of learning from one another, of sharing our strengths with one another, we can all elevate our humanity.

And mutual trust engenders a meeting of minds in the truest sense.

Though he was not a religious figure, I have great admiration for the father of modern education in Indonesia, Ki Hajar Dewantara (1889–1959).

The motto of Indonesian education, 'Support from Behind', comes from the Javanese saying: 'Those in the front provide models, those in the middle serve, and those behind provide support,' the meaning of which was emphasized by Mr Ki Hajar Dewantara.

It seems to me that SGI members, through their discussion meetings, are also striving to build such beautiful and harmonious human relationships.

**Ikeda:** I appreciate your insights into our activities.

In one of the Buddhist scriptures Shakyamuni speaks of the differing and varied temperaments and circumstances of people with the metaphor that there are lotuses with blue flowers, red flowers, and white flowers; some grow in the water, some float on its surface, and some rise above it.

Ten people will have ten different travails of which to tell; a hundred will have a hundred to tell. Our aim is to share in and challenge each hardship with our entire being so that all may enjoy a life of happiness and triumph.

Second Soka Gakkai president Josei Toda, referring to the words 'I have never for a moment neglected'[17] from the Lotus Sutra, insisted that Soka Gakkai must continue striving tirelessly to enable all suffering people, without exception, to become happy.

It was his undying wish that Soka Gakkai become a 'great earth of inspiration' for humankind.

As we move forward toward our eightieth anniversary (2010), the discussion meeting will continue to serve as the pillar of our movement as we strive to generate greater currents of peace and humanity throughout our respective communities and society in general.

# SIX

# The Spirit of Tolerance

**Ikeda:** Soka University has welcomed educational and cultural leaders from the Central Asian Islamic Republic of Uzbekistan in the past.

And since 1989 the university has been engaged in joint research on the Silk Road with the Uzbekistan Academy of Science, discovering important artefacts of Buddhist culture from the Kushan Empire (second century BCE–third century CE).

Soka University graduates who are involved in Central Asian studies, including Silk Road archeological surveys, have sent me copies of works by Ibnu Sina (980–1037), the great philosopher and physician, published in Uzbekistan.

In his writings we find the words: 'True friendship is one's golden treasure.'

My friendship with you, President Wahid, is indeed golden and glorious for its enlightening instruction. Let us continue our discussions for the sake of the future.

In July 2009, the results of a survey of long-term Japanese residents in Indonesia and other Islamic countries outside the Middle East were published.

In response to the question, 'Has your image of Islam changed since you came to the country you are now living in?' a high percentage of respondents residing in South-East Asia answered that their impression had indeed changed. The majority had positive feelings after actually interacting directly with people in Islamic societies.

Among the specific replies, one respondent commented that he had come to appreciate the purity and beauty of religious belief, and said that he was especially moved by the Pancasila (Five Moral Principles that Define the Indonesian Nation). The Pancasila were instituted when your nation was founded, weren't they?

**Wahid:** Yes. My father was a member of the Committee for Preparatory Work for Indonesian Independence (BPUPK), and was one of those responsible for the official adoption of the Pancasila as our nation's guiding principles. The five moral principles of the Pancasila are cited in the preamble to our 1945 national constitution. They are:

1. Belief in the one and only God
2. A just and civilized humanity
3. The unity of Indonesia
4. Democracy led by the wisdom of deliberations among representatives
5. Social justice for all citizens of Indonesia

The 1945 constitution guarantees freedom for the development of all religions. As far as the nation is concerned, all religious followers are equal, and they are Indonesian citizens, whatever religion they practise. They are our Indonesian brothers and sisters, and they have the right to follow the beliefs of their chosen religion and observe their religious duties.

We have a formal code for that and an ethic of valuing religious belief and peaceful coexistence.

Religious faith and peaceful coexistence serve as the framework for the unity and identity of Indonesian society as a whole. It is the duty of every member of Indonesian society to work together to preserve this harmonious and peaceful atmosphere.

I am pleased that, as the results of the survey you mentioned reveal, those who have lived for an extended length of time in Indonesia have a positive impression and have acquired a deeper understanding of our national ideals and of Islam.

**Ikeda:** As you say, it has become increasingly important for people to overcome their differences and work together for the sake of peace and the development of democratic societies.

In that regard as well, it is imperative for us to make a sincere effort to learn the truth about others who are different from ourselves.

All too frequently today, we make no effort to learn about people who are different from us but hold arbitrary, unilateral views about them based on unbalanced information and biases. This leads to the repetition of conflict and tragedy. The same is true regarding perceptions over religion.

Shakyamuni Buddha stressed the importance of seeing the world as it is. Perceiving reality truthfully is the first step.

First Soka Gakkai president Tsunesaburo Makiguchi also warned of making judgements before we appreciate the reality of a situation.

One can learn a great deal by actually visiting a country that one was not previously very knowledgeable about, participating in the life of that society, and engaging in dialogue and interacting with its people. The encounter with the history and culture in which that country takes pride can also be quite inspiring.

That is why in 1962 I established the Institute of Oriental Philosophy as a nexus for studying the cultures and philosophies of various countries, promoting scholarly exchange, and deepening mutual understanding.

The historian Arnold J. Toynbee also emphasized: 'In my experience the solvent of traditional prejudice has been personal acquaintance. When one becomes personally acquainted with a fellow human being, of whatever religion, nationality, or race, one cannot fail to recognize that he is human like oneself.'[1]

My own experience affirms Dr Toynbee's observation to the letter.

**Wahid:** I agree.

The first work of Dr Toynbee that I read was his lecture series on Islamic and Western civilization.

I also read your dialogue with Toynbee, the content of which I still find very appealing. It provided me with invaluable ideas concerning the issues that I was facing as a follower of Islam.

As a historian, Toynbee discusses how a group should react to challenges and how it can discover the best solutions to the problems it encounters.

**Ikeda:** Yes, he did. I, too, learned a great deal from Dr Toynbee in our dialogue.

The ancient Greek poet Aeschylus (525–456 BCE), whom Dr Toynbee admired, wrote: 'Wisdom comes alone through suffering.'[2]

This is the principle that the response to adversity is what stimulates the wisdom for fresh creation. And the source of that wisdom is the inner struggle of each individual to create and shape the society in which he or she lives.

Peace, too, relies on the persistent efforts of individuals in every country who, despite the arduousness of the challenge, strive with tireless tenacity to facilitate mutual understanding.

Those who see things from the narrow-minded perspective of self-interest cannot perceive the true reality of others.

Toynbee saw that one of his responsibilities as a historian was to help broaden such limiting perspectives and encourage people to overcome their self-centredness.

**Wahid:** Yes, I understand what you are saying.

The factor that causes conflict is the idea that one's own benefit is all that matters. Those who subscribe to this point of view have no tolerance for others and care only about themselves.

In your dialogue with Dr Toynbee, he stressed the need to change the selfish attitude of trying to use everything for one's own benefit and the view that one is a member of one particular society alone, with no broader loyalties.

He said that the true role of religion is to establish the truth that we are members of the human race and the universe.

**Ikeda:** Yes, precisely.

Dr Toynbee hoped that religion would become a driving force for enabling human beings to attain a proactive spirit of tolerance. As he wrote:

> In the world in which we now find ourselves, the adherents of the differ-
> ent living religions ought to be the readier to tolerate, respect, and revere
> one another's religious heritages because, in our generation, there is not
> anyone alive who is effectively in a position to judge between his own
> religion and his neighbour's.[3]

The United Nations designated 2009 as the International Year of Reconciliation and 2010 as the International Year for the Rapprochement of Cultures.

That religion has been foundational to many cultures and civilizations is undisputable. Which is why interfaith dialogue can be such a powerful force in promoting mutual understanding.

Efforts to promote dialogue between Islam and Christianity have been underway for some time. In your view, what is the most essential element for such dialogues to succeed?

**Wahid:** Mutual respect. The follower of Islam must respect Christianity, and the follower of Christianity must respect Islam. If that is the case, if there is an attitude of mutual respect, they will be able to overcome their competitive nature in a positive way.

**Ikeda:** The same is true in dialogues between Islam and Buddhism, isn't it?

At this point I would like to focus our attention on the origins of Islam and Buddhism, the lives of the Prophet Mohammed and Shakyamuni.

**Wahid:** Of course.

Mohammed is said to have been born in around 570 in the city of Mecca on the Arabian Peninsula. Though he was a member of the powerful Quraysh Tribe, his own family was not wealthy, and his father Abd Allah ibn Abd al Muttalib (545–570 CE) died before Mohammed was born. His mother also passed away when Mohammed was six years old.

He was taken into the care of his grandfather, yet even before the grief of losing his mother had healed, he, too, had died before Mohammed was eight.

In his childhood, when he should have enjoyed the love and protection of his parents, Mohammed lost not only them but also his guardian, his grandfather, becoming an orphan.

Fortunately, his uncle Abu Talib ibn Abd al-Muttalib (549–619) became Mohammed's guardian and raised him. Though their life was poor, when Mohammed was twenty-five his fortunes improved with his marriage to a leading female merchant of Mecca, Khadija bint Khuwaylid (555–619). Mohammed was serious and devoted to his work, causing him to be praised as 'Amin', meaning 'trustworthy one', and it was this that drew the attention of Khadija to him and prompted her to seek him in marriage.

A passage in the Qur'an describes these events: 'Did He not find you an orphan and shelter you, find you lost and guide you, find you in need and satisfy your need?'(Qur'an [93]:6–8).[4]

**Ikeda:** Mohammed's life, then, began with a childhood marked by loss and suffering.

Both his parents died when he was a boy. Shakyamuni also lost his mother when he was only a week old.

Shakyamuni was born as a prince in what is part of present-day Nepal. Various dates are given for his birth, as either in the sixth or fifth century BCE.

From his youth he revealed himself as an individual of extraordinary abilities, and in spite of the fact that he was raised in a protected, pampered environment, he was drawn to and thought deeply on life's problems.

It is believed that the suffering and sadness he experienced as a result of his mother's death soon after his birth was a contributing factor to his seriousness.

As he grew up into an outstanding young man, he witnessed an aged person and realized that he, too, would eventually grow old. He also came to understand that no one could escape illness and death, either.

Even after marrying and having a son, he could not dispel the profound sorrow arising from the inevitability of birth, old age, sickness, and death (the Four Sufferings in Buddhism) from his mind, and he finally decided to renounce his worldly possessions and seek the life of an ascetic.

Looking back on those events in his final year of life, Shakyamuni said that he left all that he had 'to seek the good'.[5]

Forsaking his social standing as a prince, he engaged in a personal quest for the fundamental answer to the unchanging human condition – birth, old age, sickness, and death.

The words 'to seek the good' are thought to represent his profound courage and resolve to discover the way for all people, not just himself, to triumph over suffering and find happiness.

**Wahid:** His departure from home was a great turning point in Shakyamuni's life.

**Ikeda:** Yes.

The problem of birth, old age, sickness, and death that Shakyamuni grappled with was not a problem unique to him; it is the reality confronting us all, an enduring theme of all great literature, philosophy, and religion, in every time and place.

For example, we find this passage in a drama composed by Sutan Takdir Alisjahbana (1908–94), who is widely admired as the father of modern Indonesia: 'Why are we born? Why must we die?'[6]

Why are we born and why do we die? This is the question, I believe, of the meaning of life.

When we look honestly at the reality of death, it empowers us to make our lives more fulfilling. In order to lead a life of eternal value, we must search for life's meaning.

In Alisjahbana's great work *Kalah dan Menang* (War and Love, 1978), a young boy is raised under a sternly disciplined regime instituted by Japanese militarist authorities, and comes to glorify war and praise the act of giving one's life in battle. A woman in the story tries to tell him how wonderful it is to live out his life to the utmost: 'Can't you see how beautiful life is, and that if you can live it with responsibility and a shining creativity, it becomes deeply meaningful and incredibly rich? Nothing is more beautiful or noble than to be alive.'[7]

Because life is precious and irreplaceable, even as we face the realities of birth, old age, sickness, and death, Buddhism teaches us to exercise our creativity for the sake of others and society and to lead the fullest, most ennobling life.

**Wahid:** Yes, I see.

Mohammed is known for his religious nobility, his lofty character, and his outstanding morals, as well as for his honesty as a person.

After marrying, Mohammed lived a relatively peaceful life, but even before receiving his divine call as the Prophet, he thought deeply about the evidence of the power of God – especially by observing and pondering on beauty in all its forms, power, and as Allah's creation.

Considering Heaven and Earth and all that lies between, he asked himself what harms and causes the destruction of human society and why people worship false gods.

Mount Hira on the outskirts of Mecca is a small hill that can be climbed in thirty minutes, and Mohammed went there once a year to meditate in a cave.

In 610, when Mohammed was forty years old, he received a message from the angel Jibrail (Gabriel) in the cave on Mount Hira. This event is known as Laylat al-Qadr, the Night of Power or the Night of Destiny.

In the forty years of his life up to that point, Mohammed had undergone the preparations to accept this extremely important mission, and then the angel Jibrail visited him and imparted the words of Allah to him.

The great soul of the Prophet was illuminated by the light of this divine inspiration, and he etched the words conveyed to him in his heart.

These divine messages continued for the twenty and more remaining years of the Prophet Mohammed's life, and were eventually compiled into the Qur'an.

**Ikeda:** If I'm not mistaken, then, the various hardships that Mohammed underwent in the forty years before he accepted his extremely important mission prepared him for the task, and thus they all had a profound significance.

Shakyamuni, who abandoned his worldly possessions and began his quest to seek the answers to the fundamental problems of human existence – birth, old age, sickness, and death – initially practised strict austerities in the forest, including a regimen of fasting. This was based on the idea prevalent in India at the time that in order to attain spiritual purity, one had to punish the impure body and weaken it.

But after pursuing such austerities for six years without attaining enlightenment, Shakyamuni realized that they were not the path to truth, and he abandoned them. He then calmed both his body and mind and entered into a state of meditation under a bodhi tree at Boddhagaya, reflecting deeply on his innermost being.

This delving into the deepest realms of his inner being transcended the levels of life associated with one's family, ethnic group, the human race, and the natural world, the levels of the Earth, and the Milky Way; it reached as deep as the fundamental origins of the universe itself and ultimately became inseparable with the life of the entire cosmos.

In this insight into the inner universe, Shakyamuni discovered the true reality of the universe that all living beings are interrelated and interconnected as they repeat the timeless cycle of birth and death.

He declared that ignorance, in the form of egoism, rooted deep within the recesses of all living beings, is the cause of the sufferings brought on by birth, old age, sickness, and death.

Having broken through this fundamental ignorance, Shakyamuni awakened to the fundamental Law, or truth, that permeates the life of the entire universe. One who has awakened to that eternal Law is called a Buddha. Later, Nichiren entitled that Law *Nam-myoho-renge-kyo*.

The life of the Buddha, who has awakened to the cosmic Law, is filled with the wisdom and compassion rising forth from the life force of the universe and possesses the capacity to transform the sufferings of birth, old age, sickness, and death into great joy. He then acts to relieve the suffering of all living beings.

The aim of Buddhism is to summon forth this life of the Buddha that exists within all humanity. It is a religion of awakening founded on the fundamental Law of the universe, a religion of wisdom, and a religion of compassion.

**Wahid:** What actions did Shakyamuni take after attaining enlightenment?

**Ikeda:** A strict caste system existed in the India of Shakyamuni's day. In tandem with the caste system, the prevailing philosophy of karma held that one's destiny was predetermined, and no amount of effort on one's part could change it.

In addition, among the Brahman caste prior to Shakyamuni, in most cases only a few of the most advanced disciples were given access to the highest teachings.

It was against this background of a restrictive caste system and a philosophy of predetermined karma that Shakyamuni expounded that all human beings could tap the inner life condition of the Buddha. This was a remarkable breakthrough.

As I noted earlier, Shakyamuni first shared his teachings not with society's rulers but with the five friends with whom he had been practising austerities in the forest. He walked 250 kilometres from the place where he had attained enlightenment to Sarnath, where his friends were.

According to scholarly research, Shakyamuni preached his teachings more than 900 times in one Indian kingdom, more than 120 times in a city in another kingdom, and forty-nine times in a city of another kingdom. He consistently reached out to share his teachings for the sake of others.

Until his death at the age of eighty in a grove of sal trees, he taught many things.

He extended his compassion equally to all who came to him in search of instruction.

The Lotus Sutra stands as the epitome of Shakyamuni's many scriptures, which collectively are often described as 'the eighty thousand teachings'. In the Sutra, he declared his intent to teach all people so they may attain enlightenment equal to his own, and in no respect different.[8]

This means that he wished to elevate all humanity to a state of being identical to his own.

Islam is also a world religion, open to all people without discrimination based on social status or ethnicity. Mohammed's wife, Khadija, was the first convert to Islam, wasn't she?

**Wahid:** Yes. At a time when no one would listen to the words of Allah communicated to them by the Prophet Mohammed, it was his wife Khadija who first accepted the teachings.

Khadija not only provided the financial support needed for Mohammed to propagate his teachings, but always remained close by his side, enduring the threats made to Mohammed from those who opposed Islam and providing an outstanding example for all female followers of Islam in later times.

Mohammed was deeply grateful to Khadija, saying that because of her noble, virtuous spirit, she was certain to be born a queen in her future life.

In contrast, his uncle Abu Talib continued to support and protect Mohammed, but he never converted to Islam.

Yet Mohammed continued to live with and cherish his uncle, demonstrating the principle of accepting diversity.

In addition, when three Christian priests visited Mohammed from Najran (a region in eastern Saudi Arabia), Mohammed allowed them to pray in the mosque.

As I mentioned earlier, Mohammed received the teaching from Allah concerning differences of religious belief, 'you have your religion and I have mine' (Qur'an [109]:6).[9] Islam teaches a spirit of tolerance, in which we must respect others as fellow human beings, even if they follow a different religion.

**Ikeda:** The majority of religions have at their foundation such respect for others and tolerance.

Shakyamuni declared his wish that all living beings should enjoy happiness, tranquility, and ease: 'May all be well and secure, May all beings be happy!'[10]

Buddhism also articulates several principles for living a correct life, including refraining from taking life, lying, greed, and views that distort the truth.

It is noteworthy that refraining from taking life is the first of these principles.

Nonviolence is a core component of Buddhism.

Interestingly, the founders of the great world religions, not only Mohammed and Shakyamuni but also Moses and Jesus, all underwent great hardship throughout the course of their lives.

Shakyamuni's life was threatened on numerous occasions.

Devadatta, Shakyamuni's cousin and follower who was driven by personal ambition, grew jealous of and betrayed Shakyamuni.

He rolled a boulder down a mountain to kill Shakyamuni, and tricked a king into releasing his elephants to trample Shakyamuni.

He also tried to sow division among Shakyamuni's followers, encouraging some of them to denounce their teacher. The plot was thwarted by two of the Buddha's leading disciples, Shariputra and Maudgalyayana.

Others also tried to cause Shakyamuni's downfall by spreading false charges against him. On one occasion he was accused of being the instigator of a murder, though he was able to prove his innocence.

The Lotus Sutra states: 'Since hatred and jealousy toward this sutra abound even when the thus come one is in the world, how much more will this be so after his passing?'[11]

Those who are speaking out for what is true and just are always the targets of baseless persecution and defamation.

Nichiren declared: 'Worthies and sages are tested by abuse.'[12]

The true greatness of a sage or saint is revealed by their behaviour when persecuted. I believe we must not overlook this fact when striving to understand the essential character of a religion.

**Wahid:** Precisely.

With the support of his relatives, Mohammed began his propagation activities in the area around Mecca, but the persecutions he faced increased in proportion to the growth in the number of his followers.

The head of the Quraysh tribe, fearing control of Mecca would fall into the hands of Mohammed, obstinately tried to obstruct him at every turn. The Quraysh also enacted a boycott against Mohammed's followers, forcing them into starvation, while also continuing to attack them militarily, resorting to every means at their disposal to halt the growth of the followers of Islam.

In 619, in the midst of this bitter struggle, Mohammed was struck by the tragic loss of both his wife, who had been a precious source of support, and his uncle Abu Talib, who had protected the Prophet.

With the death of Abu Talib, who as head of the Hasyim family had been a staunch protector of the propagation of Islam, the unbelieving Quraysh tribe became more daring in their attempts to stop Mohammed.

At the gathering during which the Quraysh tribe in Mecca hatched a plot to assassinate Mohammed by night, Mohammed's own Hasyim family was placed in a position where they could not avenge Mohammed's death, because representatives of all the tribes were present.

But the angel Jibrail informed Mohammed of the upcoming attack, enabling him to escape in time.

Then, receiving the command of Allah, in 622 Mohammed and his followers went to Yathrib (later Medina), a distance of more than 300 kilometres from Mecca.

This event, the Hijra, marks the beginning of the Islamic calendar.

Before departing for Yathrib, Mohammed sent a messenger. The people of Yathrib were virtuous, and they pledged that they were prepared to shoulder the responsibility of protecting Mohammed. Mohammed then moved to Yathrib, where he cherished the people, and in particular, the minorities.

The move of Mohammed to Yathrib marks the early period of the birth of Islamic civilization.

**Ikeda:** In the midst of adversity, then, Mohammed moved to Yathrib, where he would bring harmony to the people, freeing them from the spectre of the tribal loyalties that engendered conflict while working to establish a communal framework based on the Islamic faith.

As I said previously, there was no discrimination among the followers of Shakyamuni, either based on ethnicity or social class, or between the monks and the laity.

Shakyamuni said: 'Do not ask about descent, but ask about conduct; from [any] wood, it is true, fire is born: likewise a firm Muni (i.e., a sage or religious saint), although belonging to a low family, may become noble, when restrained from sinning by humility.'[13]

As these words reveal, the order of Shakyamuni's followers was a gathering of individuals striving in their practice with a shared aim, without any distinctions based on birth or social status.

Am I correct to understand that there is no professional clergy in Islam?

**Wahid:** No, there is not.

The Qur'an instructs against discriminating against the followers of Islam in these words: 'But God will give [due] rewards to those who believe in Him and His messengers and make no distinction between any of them. God is most forgiving and merciful' (Qur'an [4]:152).[14]

An interesting episode is recorded after the Hijra, when Mohammed was living with his followers in Yathrib.

The first thing that Mohammed undertook after moving to Yathrib was to build a mosque at a place known as al-Masjid an Nabawi (the Prophet's Mosque), which is still visited by many Muslims to this day. In constructing the first building on that site, it is said, Mohammed joined with his followers in carrying the sun-dried bricks for the mosque.

There is a passage in the Qur'an that explicates, for many followers of Islam, the kind of person Mohammed was: 'A Messenger has come to you from among yourselves. Your suffering distresses him: he is deeply concerned for you and full of kindness and mercy towards the believers'(Qur'an [9]:128).[15]

And in describing their faith, the Qur'an states: '[Believers], you are the best community singled out for people: you order what is right, forbid what is wrong, and believe in God. If the People of the Book had also believed, it would have been better for them. For although some of them do believe, most of them are lawbreakers' (Qur'an [3]:110).[16]

**Ikeda:** In that sense, the two world religions Islam and Buddhism both grieve over the plight of others and share the noble spirit of offering relief to the people as foundational beliefs.

I'd like to introduce several anecdotes on Shakyamuni that shed light on these points.

A sick man had been left for dead by all and was suffering in solitude. Shakyamuni went to his side, gently patted the dirtied man to soothe him, bathed him, and changed his bedding.

Some of those around Shakyamuni wondered why he, such an eminent personage, should personally care for the ailing man, but Shakyamuni told them, 'If you wish to serve the Buddha, care for the sick.'

When the Buddhist order was founded, the Buddha and his followers wore the robes of the poorest and lowliest members of society.

One day a leading disciple of the Buddha, who was blind, was trying to darn his tattered robe but found it impossible to thread the needle.

The man who approached him to help was his teacher, Shakyamuni. When the disciple protested, Shakyamuni is said to have explained that he, too, wished to continue to accumulate good fortune.

The anecdote shows that even the Buddha can never know rest in the task of caring for others and accumulating good fortune.

Another story tells of Shakyamuni meeting a woman caught in the throes of grief because her beloved child had died and how he encouraged her to overcome her sorrow. Throughout his life, Shakyamuni never stopped actively reaching out to help people triumph over suffering.

Buddhism teaches that 'The varied sufferings that all living beings undergo – all these are the Thus Come One's own sufferings.'[17] Sharing the distress of others as if it were one's own is elemental to Buddhism.

This is why Shakyamuni taught his followers to work among the people for the sake of their welfare and well-being. Those who strive, based on the teachings of the Buddha, to respect and value the lives of others and who place the highest priority on alleviating their sufferings, are called bodhisattvas.

Bodhisattvas make four universal vows.

The first is to save innumerable living beings. This has two aspects – the religious mission of enabling all people to manifest the life state of the Buddha within them, and the social mission of contributing to the prosperity of the community and the peace of humankind.

The second is to eradicate every earthly desire. This entails overcoming all one's negative, evil thoughts and desires and transforming them into goodness and virtue to help others.

The third is to master every Buddhist teaching. In contemporary terms, it is the determination to study the intellectual heritage of humanity, from Buddhism to all fields of learning, philosophy, and religion.

The fourth vow is to attain supreme enlightenment. Through one's practice to aid others, one strengthens one's own goodness and brings forth one's life state of the Buddha.

Today, both Soka Gakkai and SGI are the heirs to this bodhisattva way, striving to advance a movement promoting peace, culture and education worldwide.

Additionally, Mahatma Gandhi (1869–1948) can be cited among those individuals who embodied Shakyamuni's teaching of compassion and nonviolence in the twentieth century.

I know you have a profound regard for Gandhi, President Wahid.

**Wahid:** Yes. Gandhi is famous for the journeys he made on foot. I have visited Gandhi's grave in India. After being felled by an assassin's bullet, Gandhi was cremated at Raj Ghat in Delhi. Hundreds of thousands are said to have gathered for the occasion.

On our way back from visiting Gandhi's grave, I stressed to my daughter Yenny Zannuba Wahid how vast Gandhi's influence was, to the extent that such multitudes had come to pay their last respects to him. I asked her to consider the Prophet Mohammed, too, whose name 800 million people recite on a daily basis. That, I said to her, is the power of the human spirit.

**Ikeda:** I have also visited Raj Ghat and offered flowers at Gandhi's memorial. On my second visit, I wrote in the visitor's log: 'The father of the country sleeps here. / The people visit and pay their respects. / I pray for the eternal happiness / Of father and children alike.'

Gandhi made the point that Mohammed, Shakyamuni, and Christ were each, in their own distinct ways, champions of peace.

With regard to the relationship between Gandhi and Shakyamuni, Gandhi wrote in a letter that '[W]hen in 1890 or 1891, I became acquainted with the teaching of the Buddha, my eyes were opened to the limitless possibilities of nonviolence.'[18]

Gandhi also evidenced a deep interest in the philosophy and life of Nichiren, and incorporated chanting *Nam-myoho-renge-kyo* as part of his daily prayers.

From these things we can see that Gandhi had an open and accepting mind with regard to other religions.

**Wahid:** Yes. Gandhi made a concerted effort to promote interfaith dialogue.

I am a follower of Islam, but I am also a believer in Gandhism – in other words, someone dedicated to the philosophy advocated by Gandhi.

Islam seeks to bring peace.

Gandhi also stressed, 'Nonviolence is the law of our species as violence is the law of the brute.'[19] His philosophy of nonviolence should be adopted by all humanity.

**Ikeda:** I agree completely.

Every religion, while following its own teachings and doctrines, should ask itself how it may best contribute to peace and the welfare of individuals and society. I believe actions centred on the human being are particularly important at this time.

It is said that when Shakyamuni was eighty years old, he spoke to the minister of a powerful kingdom planning to invade another state and in discussing the principles that lead nations to prosperity or decline, he eventually persuaded the minister not to launch an invasion and thereby prevented a war.

A certain king extolled Shakyamuni, saying, 'Those whom we, with weapons, cannot force to surrender, you subdue unarmed.'[20]

Only through dialogue and language can we find the way to nonviolence.

You have also been a great champion of words.

**Wahid:** You honour me.

I have opposed dictatorial government and summoned the courage to write for the sake of truth and justice. This is because I was raised from my youth by my grandfather and father to embody the honesty of a leader of a *pesantren*.

Honesty is a relative quality, but the important thing is to be honest at all times. I cannot lie, whether I want to or not. This requires tremendous courage.

**Ikeda:** True courage is persisting in the path of nonviolence, through dialogue and by speaking out for truth and justice. That is the path of valour taken by the valorous.

Soon after World War II, Gandhi cited the kingdom of the ancient Indian monarch Ashoka (304–232 BCE) as an example of a realm based on nonviolence.

King Ashoka of the ancient Indian Maurya Empire (323–185 BCE) was an ardent follower of Buddhism who declared that victory through the Law (the Buddhist teachings) was true victory, superior to that won by force of arms.

He renounced war and engaged in such initiatives as building hospitals to promote the people's welfare in manifold ways – not only in his own realm but in neighbouring realms as well.

One of Ashoka's famous edicts declares that he exerts himself in every area for the benefit of the people.[21]

This is a spirit that seems to have much in common with your beliefs as a wise political leader, President Wahid.

**Wahid:** To me, politics is working as hard as one can for the welfare of the people.

**Ikeda:** Another of Ashoka's edicts states: 'all religions should reside everywhere.'[22] This is also consonant with the spirit of tolerance that you uphold, President Wahid.

Acting upon the Buddhist spirit of tolerance, Ashoka protected the freedom of all religions, embraced every ethnic and national group, and strove to create a flourishing spiritual culture.

Moreover, he sent emissaries of peace to such distant lands in the west as Macedonia, Syria, and Egypt in an effort to facilitate international philosophical and cultural exchange. He established relations with Greek kings and recognized the achievements of Hellenistic civilization. Such moves, some have noted, led to certain Buddhist influences finding their way into Judaism and early Christianity.

Another of Ashoka's edicts states: 'There is no better work than promoting the welfare of all the people.'[23]

King Kanishka (127–151 CE) of the later Kushan Empire carried forward Ashoka's Buddhist spirit of tolerance.

The Kushan Empire unified a vast territory that included India, Iran, and Central Asia. Upholding the principle of freedom of religious belief, it promoted a lively exchange between the peoples of East and West, helping to bring them together.

Mahayana Buddhism flourished in this region of remarkable diversity and international exchange. This Buddhist school sought to return to Shakyamuni's original spirit and serve as a 'great vehicle' to deliver all people to enlightenment.

The Buddhist teacher and poet Ashvagosha (80–150 CE), a spiritual mentor of King Kanishka, wrote that one must regard all living beings only with love and compassion, never regard them with anger or harm, and hold aloft the torch of this teaching for them.[24]

Mahayana Buddhism gradually spread to the other countries of Asia, and on to China and Japan.

It was also at this time that there was a great blossoming of thought. The melding of Grecian and Indian civilizations led to important new developments in science and art, including philosophy, astronomy, medicine, and other areas. One particularly noteworthy example is Gandharan art.

Later, from the fifth through the twelfth century, the great Buddhist university of Nalanda flourished as a centre of Buddhist learning.

At its height, thousands of scholars gathered there and, in a vibrant atmosphere of intellectual exploration, more than a hundred lectures were held on a daily basis. Such Chinese Buddhist monks as Xuanzang (602–64) and I-Ching (Yijing; 635–713) risked their lives travelling to Nalanda to study.

**Wahid:** As we have already mentioned, there was interaction between Indonesia and Nalanda, and I-Ching visited Indonesia. It has also been confirmed that Gandharan art reached Indonesia.

Islam has a history of an open spirit of absorbing the wisdom and knowledge of many different peoples of the world.

And Islamic civilization was created in a pluralistic society encompassing the believers of many religions, such as Judaism, Christianity, Hinduism, and Chinese religious beliefs.

For example, Harun Ar-Rasyid (also Harun al-Rashid; 763–809), the fifth caliph of the Abbasid Caliphate (758–1258), protected and supported various traditions of learning as he built the foundations for Islamic civilization to flourish.

He had the library known as the Hijannatul al-Hikmah, 'The Treasure House of Learning', constructed in Baghdad.

His son Al-Ma'mun Ar-Rasyid (786–833) went on to develop the library into Bayt al-Hikmah, the academy known as the 'Tower of Learning'.

The library is said to have been the largest in the world at the time, and it became a centre for translating Greek and Syrian manuscripts on a wide variety of subjects into Arabic. Through this translation project, which began in the early ninth century, a vast amount of knowledge became available in Arabic to the educated classes of Islamic civilization and, combined with the rich wisdom of Islam, emerged as a new, comprehensive system of knowledge.

**Ikeda:** That is an important historical development.

At the time, Baghdad, known as 'the capital of peace', was also a great centre of publishing and literary activity.

The famous catalogue of books published by the tenth-century bookseller Ibnu al-Nadim (936–95) lists an exceptionally wide range of works, including Buddhist, Jewish, Christian, and Greek texts, as well as works on Chinese philosophy, and world philosophy, literature, history, and science.

The renowned Abbasid Caliphate poet Al-Muntanabbi (915–65)

praised the value of books as well, calling them a partner most conversant with world affairs.

Fostering a healthy culture of the written word serves as a foundation for enriching human nature and building a better society.

**Wahid:** Yes, it's vital.

I am always aware of the importance, in order to prevent the decline of the culture of the written word, of creating an environment that enables as many as possible to have access to good books.

Our civilization has been able to advance thus far because of the written word. Not only can it capture our thoughts and feelings, but it preserves them for the ages and allows us to revisit them again and again. In other words, the written word has the quality of continuity.

Even after I lost my sight, I continue to enjoy books in every form and strive to learn from all kinds of books.

I remember as a boy I often used to ride my bicycle to the library. That location has now, however, become a shopping mall.

There are public libraries throughout Japan, where citizens can borrow books free of charge, aren't there?

In Indonesia, books are still quite expensive, so I hope that the government will take measures reducing taxes on books or exempting them from taxation, to help keep their price down.

I also would like to see the government build more public libraries and rental lending libraries, to promote people's desire to read.

**Ikeda:** Books were luxury items in Japan for many years in the past as well. During World War II, I would bring some of my most precious books with me to the air-raid shelter during attacks. After the war, I still couldn't afford new books, so I frequented the Kanda area of Tokyo, Japan's largest used-book district.

When there was a book I really wanted, I use to scrape together the cost from my meagre salary and dash to the bookstore, feeling tremendously relieved if it was still there, then rush home with it tucked safely under my arm.

Today, with the popularity of such visual media as television, as well as the advances in computers and their widespread adoption, the shift away from print media has become cause for growing dismay.

My friend the American economist Lester C. Thurow expressed his concern to me that when we rely too heavily on visual media, we tend to react viscerally and emotionally.

**Wahid:** The majority of people are today shifting to the computer, and I think that after a while we will see a shift to a civilization based on a balance between the printed word and internet. This is an important development.

As an example of the kind of Indonesian literature I would like to recommend to young people, there is the excellent book by Mochtar Lubis (1922–2004) entitled *A Road with No End*. And of the writings of the great Pramoedya Ananta Toer (1925–2006), I would suggest *This Earth of Mankind, Child of All Nations, Footsteps,* and *House of Glass.*

Another Indonesian writer on a par with Pramoedya is Ahmad Tohari (b. 1948). I feel his three-volume work *The Dancer* is one of his masterpieces.

There are so many fine books worth reading.

**Ikeda:** Yes, that is very true.

Books are the sustenance for our education.

Islamic civilization has made important contributions to education, historically.

What was the focus of education and scholarship in Baghdad during the Abbasid Caliphate?

**Wahid:** The madrasah, an institution attached to the mosque, was responsible for education. It taught the Qur'an and various other scholarly subjects.

There the instructor sat in a chair and his pupils sat around him at his feet, listening to his lecture.

The famous Madrasah Nizamiyyah was built in Baghdad in the eleventh century. The building that housed the Madrasah Mustansiriyyah, built in the thirteenth century, still survives today.

Al-Azhar University in Cairo, where I studied, precedes both of those, having been established in the tenth century. It has a long and hallowed history.

Many studied there, engaged in the pursuit of knowledge through Arabic translations of numerous manuscripts, including the philosophical works of Aristotle (384–322 BCE) and Plato (427–347 BCE) and the medical writings of Hippocrates (460– c.370 BCE).

Al-Kindi (c.801–66), author of *On the Intellect,* and Al-Farabi (c.870–950) were pioneers in philosophical studies in the Islamic world.

Somewhat later came Ibn Sina (980–1037) and Ibn Rushd (1126–98), who were well known in medieval Europe.

Other scholars made important contributions to mathematics and science, such as Muhammad ibn Musa al-Khawarizmi (780–850), who invented a method of calculation employing Arabic numbers, and Ibn al-Haytham (965–1040), who discovered the structure of the eye.

As a result, Islamic civilization was a cradle of culture and science from the ninth through the thirteenth centuries. The knowledge accumulated by Islamic scholars was transmitted to Europe and formed the cornerstone of the Renaissance that began there in the fourteenth century – a historical fact that is perhaps not very widely known.

**Ikeda:** That's true. The far-reaching work of Islamic scholars in translation as well as in science and culture played a major role in the flowering of the Renaissance in Europe.

Earlier we were talking about how knowledge from other cultures was translated into Arabic and incorporated into Islamic civilization. In Buddhism, the translation of the Buddhist scriptures was also conducted on a sweeping scale.

Shakyamuni's lifetime of teachings were assembled into an enormous body of texts, which were transmitted from India through Central Asia along the Silk Road, arriving in China at about the beginning of the Common Era.

At that stage, the Chinese actively engaged in an effort to translate the Buddhist scriptures into Chinese. Kumarajiva is perhaps the best known of the great translators.

**Wahid:** Which scriptures did Kumarajiva translate?

**Ikeda:** The most famous is the Lotus Sutra (in eight volumes). He also translated the Vimalakirti Sutra (in three volumes), the Larger Wisdom Sutra (in twenty-seven volumes), the Treatise on the Great Perfection of Wisdom (in 100 volumes), and the Treatise on the Middle Way (in four volumes).

A national academy set up specifically to translate the Buddhist scriptures was established outside the Chinese capital of Chang'an. Kumarajiva arrived in Chang'an in 401, and together with pupils and assistants, engaged in translation efforts at the academy.

In the subsequent Tang dynasty (618–907), Buddhism – based on the body of scriptures translated into Chinese – spread from the imperial court to become a religion of the people, exerting a significant influence not only on Chinese philosophy but also on politics, science, literature, and the arts.

The Tang dynasty was also known as an especially cosmopolitan era in Chinese history when China embraced a diversity of ethnic groups, cultures, and religions, resulting in the flourishing of an open and pluralistic culture.

Many discoveries were made in China during the Tang dynasty. Among them advances in the production of paper and printing press know-how had a major impact around the world.

There were printing presses in Chang'an and other major population centres, which printed books on agriculture and medicine as well as works from the Buddhist canon.

There was considerable mutual interaction and influence among Buddhism and the native Chinese philosophies of Taoism and Confucianism, which would become the foundation of East Asian culture as a whole.

I would like to mention one Buddhist teacher in particular, Zhiyi (538–97, also known as Tiantai, from the location of the monastery at which he taught), who lived prior to the Tang dynasty and played a pivotal role in Buddhist history.

With the translation into Chinese of great numbers of scriptures and Buddhist texts, the Chinese began to compare and rank the various writings in a classification system, from which numerous orders of Buddhism, including the Tiantai, Flower Garland, Three Treatises and Zen schools, emerged. Many of these Buddhist schools were later transmitted to the Korean Peninsula and Japan.

Tiantai, whose name is often affixed with the honorific 'Great Teacher', established the Lotus Sutra as the central Buddhist scripture and was a pioneering figure in Chinese Buddhism.

Tiantai systematized the many different teachings of Buddhism, asserted that the Lotus Sutra was the supreme Buddhist teaching, and, drawing on the Lotus Sutra, established the principle of 'three thousand realms in a single moment of life.'

Simply put, this principle holds that the 'Buddha nature', in accord with the underlying, fundamental Law of the universe, exists within every individual and that each moment of life encompasses the universe itself, meaning the macrocosm and the microcosm are essentially inseparable.

In this way he established the rational basis for all living beings existing in the real world of the inescapable sufferings of birth, ageing, illness, and death to attain the expansive life state of the Buddha, equally and without distinctions.

The Lotus Sutra and the teachings of Tiantai were transmitted to Japan by Dengyo (767–822), who is also honoured with the title 'Great Teacher'. They were subsequently developed and rearticulated as a school of Buddhism for all people by Nichiren, whose teachings Soka Gakkai and SGI embrace today.

Nichiren defined the enlightenment of Shakyamuni and the essence of the Lotus Sutra, as well as the fundamental Law at the core of Tiantai's teachings, as *Nam-myoho-renge-kyo*. He also revealed a specific method for all people to manifest the wisdom and compassion inherent in the Buddha nature from within each of our lives.

By putting those teachings into practice, we, as members of the SGI, carry out our 'human revolution', the transformation of our lives from within, and engage in the effort to advance peace and prosperity in society.

I have always regarded India, China, and Korea, the nations through which Buddhism was transmitted to Japan, as our great cultural benefactors, and striven to promote cordial exchanges with them out of profound appreciation.

One must never forget the gifts bestowed from other cultures, or the history of interaction and communication. That is, I believe, a requirement when conducting dialogue among civilizations in a spirit of mutual respect.

In that sense, the great contributions of Islamic civilization to the world in the area of medicine must always be remembered and appreciated.

**Wahid:** The advancement of medicine and medical treatment within Islamic civilization is an important historical fact.

From about the ninth century, hospitals were established in Baghdad and other major centres throughout the empire, and all residents, regardless of their religion, had access to free medical care.

A comprehensive system of medical treatment for a wide range of diseases was developed, including the invention of medical instruments and a working knowledge of anaesthesiology.

Development of the medical treatment was supported by Islamic faith, as we can see from the beliefs of the eleventh-century physician Ibn Sina. His *Canon of Medicine* was a standard of medical science in Europe for several centuries.

**Ikeda:** That is a remarkable historical fact.

When we look back on history, we see that religious teachings and a sense of religious mission or duty were a driving force in the development of medicine.

Buddhism also accords medicine the highest respect.

It is said that the great physician Jivaka was Shakyamuni's personal physician. Jivaka is said to have conducted surgery to remove intestinal blockages and brain tumours, partly because he had discovered the art of fully sedating patients at this very early time in history. He was so skilled at curing serious illnesses that he was hailed as 'the king of physicians'.

The name Jivaka derives from Sanskrit meaning 'vigorous' or 'to impart life'. Physicians strengthen our life force, impart to us the vigor to live vibrantly, and lengthen our lives. They play a noble and profound role.

One of the definitions of compassion in Buddhism is 'removing suffering and giving joy'.

In the seventh century, the Tang dynasty Chinese physician Sun Simiao (581–682) stressed the importance, based on the Buddhist virtue of compassion, of regarding the suffering of the ill as one's own suffering and worked to save all from pain, regardless of their social status, wealth or poverty, age, ethnicity, or whether friend or foe.

There are no borders or discrimination in respect of the worth and dignity of life. What makes medicine a sacred calling is its dedication to saving life.

I believe that several of the leaders who founded the Indonesian Republic also happened to be physicians as well.

**Wahid:** You're referring to the origins of the University of Indonesia as a medical school, aren't you?

As you know, President Ikeda, the University of Indonesia began as the Sekolah Dokter Jawa (Java School of Medicine) in 1849. It developed from there, becoming the School tot Opleiding van Inlandsche Artsen (STOVIA), which graduated many of modern Indonesia's leaders and great thinkers.

The leader of the Budi Utomo (Noble Endeavour), the first Indonesian nationalist organization, was Sutomo (Bung Tomo, 1920–81), a physician who graduated from STOVIA.

Deeply concerned with the plight of the Indonesian people, Sutomo often treated patients at no charge, and also participated in the new nationalist movement.

Pramoedya has said of him: 'After all, most of those promoting the awakening of Asia were doctors.'[25] He also said: '[In Asia the awakening was inflamed by] the awareness that society was sick and must be cured . . .'[26] This is what inspired them. Sun Yat-sen (1866–1925) of China and José Rizal (1861–96) of the Philippines, both leaders of the independence process in their respective countries, also studied medicine.

**Ikeda:** Yes, that's right.

The words 'society was sick and must be cured' express a noble and deeply moving sense of mission.

To heal illness, lead a healthy life, and build a sound and prosperous society are aspirations universal to all humankind, transcending our differences. Therein lies the foundation of tolerance and acceptance.

And speaking of tolerance, in light of the history of peaceful co-existence between Islam and other religions, we should note the policy that allowed the followers of religions other than Islam (known as *dzimmi*, non-Muslims) living within Islamic states to govern themselves, with the payment of a special tax. We see this as well in the Ottoman Empire policy of *millets* (confessional communities), which recognized the autonomy of separate religious groups with regard to personal law.

From today's perspective, what significance do you find in such policies?

**Wahid:** From the time of Mohammed, followers of Christianity and Judaism, as 'People of the Book', were allowed to practise their faith as non-Muslims, as long as they paid a head tax known as *jizyah* and did not attack Islam. Policies were also established to protect their lives and their goods.

Later, as the area ruled by Islamic empires expanded, these policies were subsequently augmented to include Buddhists and the followers of religions other than Christianity and Judaism.

There were, however, limited exceptions, and sometimes, under oppressive governments in certain regions, followers of other religions were oppressed and persecuted, in violation of these basic principles.

The policy of recognizing non-Muslims, from today's criteria, can be evaluated in various ways, but I think it suited the forms of society in those times.

Rather than focusing on the positive and negative aspects of those historical policies, I think it is important to learn the lessons of striving for multifaith, multiethnic societies and the value of tolerance from the spirit of peaceful coexistence underlying them.

**Ikeda:** Yes, I agree.

The richness that arises from difference – in other words, diversity in cultures and civilizations – has long been an invigorating force for society, driving it forward and opening up new social eras.

The United Nations 'Human Development Report 2004 – Cultural Liberty in Today's Diverse World' states:

> The hard lines that have recently been drawn to give shape to the fear of a clash of civilizations are especially blind to world history. [. . .] The diversity of traditions within distinct civilizations is effectively ignored, and major global interventions in science, technology, mathematics and literature over millennia are made to disappear so as to give credence to a parochial view of the uniqueness of Western civilization.[27]

This is an important truth that warrants proper recognition.

**Wahid:** When I attended an international symposium in Tokyo (in November 1994), I met and spoke with Samuel Huntington, author of *The Clash of Civilizations*.

Huntington has said that in the post-Cold War world, we are seeking the answer to who we are in the values and customs of our civilizations, and that the most dangerous conflicts in the future will arise from intercultural conflict. He expressed his opinion that in the postwar world the greatest division for the West was the Iron Curtain. Now it is the difference between Western Christianity and Islam.

In opposition to that viewpoint, at the symposium I stated that it is not a question of whether differences between civilizations create clashes; such clashes are not caused by differences in lifestyles but by political and economic interests. The problem arises when one civilization attempts to impose its values on another, which never succeeds.

There is no necessity for civilizations to clash just because they are different. And if they do clash, it is usually the result of misunderstandings or prejudices rather than their actual differences.

I remember Dr Huntington listening to what I had to say, nodding in agreement. We need to make the effort to see that differences do not lead to conflict.

The important thing is to respect our mutual differences and accept the diversity and plurality of the existing reality.

King Aji Saka of the ancient Indonesian Maran kingdom said that if we wish for peace, we must respect one another.

At the Wahid Institute, we have the motto 'Seeding Plural and

Peaceful Islam', expressing our duty to promote the plurality and diversity that are the cornerstones of peace.

**Ikeda:** I agree completely with the views you've expressed.

In September 1993, at roughly the same time that Dr Huntington published his work on the clash of civilizations, I was invited to deliver an address at Harvard University. It was my second time to do so. My speech on that occasion was titled 'Mahayana Buddhism and Twenty-First Century Civilization'.

Stating my disagreement with Dr Huntington that religion is the cause of clashes between civilizations, I suggested that seeking to overcome an obsession with our differences is the springboard for a religion to become a world religion, and that open dialogue conducted in an open-minded, accepting spirit is a necessary provision for religion in the twenty-first century.

In order to explore this vision of religion, the Ikeda Center for Peace, Learning, and Dialogue in Boston, which I founded, published a book entitled *Subverting Hatred: The Challenge of Nonviolence in Religious Traditions*. In it, scholars from various religious traditions discussed the philosophy of peace articulated in Islam, Christianity, Buddhism, and five other major religions. Since its publication in 1998, it has come to be adopted as a text for courses at a number of American universities and colleges.

Professor William L. Scotty McLennan of Stanford University, one of the instructors employing *Subverting Hatred* in his classes, has said that as with human beings, religions have both positive and negative aspects. They can be exploited for political and ideological ends and abused to marginalize or even demonize other peoples and cultures. Because of that, he believed it is crucial to focus on the positive aspects of religion that foster harmony and inspire a vision of hope for the future.

The United Nations report I referred to earlier also makes the point that we should not ascribe the spread of hatred and intolerance worldwide to any one people or religion.

In that regard, the recent trend to label Islam a violent religion and the upsurge in Islamophobia among certain elements are extremely unfortunate and regrettable developments.

The European Union has compiled a list of terms that its member nations should avoid in order not to contribute to prejudice against Islam.

It calls for the disuse of terminology that associates Islam with terrorism, and to eschew the use of such words as *jihad*, which has been widely misunderstood since the September 11, 2001 attacks on the United States.

**Wahid:** This is also one of my very deep concerns.

The original meaning of jihad is to strive or make an effort.

The jihad conducted by Mohammed was a propagation effort to lead people away from pantheism to the single truth of Allah, and in that sense it actually meant to strive tirelessly to communicate the truth of Allah to others.

It is extremely dangerous to stray from that essential meaning and interpret jihad as actual war to protect religion, or as warfare against non-believers.

The essential spirit of jihad is to act with sincerity in accord with Islamic Law.

Islam is not a violent religion. It places great importance on love, and the Qur'an forbids the use of force for the sake of religion.

In converting outsiders to Islam, it is the duty of Islam's followers to do so by winning people over through the power of wisdom and eloquent sermons.

**Ikeda:** As you have consistently advocated, a world religion is one that upholds and promotes a message of peace and humanitarianism, a force facilitating acceptance of and tolerance for those with differing beliefs.

**Wahid:** Yes, precisely.

In my own life, I have always understood and respected the positions of those of different religious and cultural backgrounds and striven to build solidarity with them. The Nahdlatul Ulama (NU) has also sought to be an example of peace and harmonious coexistence for Indonesian society.

That is why it has never been our aim to make Indonesia an Islamic state. We adopted this approach from the outset. At our conference in 1935, we issued a statement saying that as followers of Islam whose faith is strong and based on our sense of morality, we do not believe it is necessary for a united Indonesia to be an Islamic state.

Being an upright religious practitioner promotes peace. As for what makes an upright religious practitioner, I believe it is a conviction in the truths of the religion you follow and an affirmation of the spirit of humanitarianism.

# SEVEN

# Education, the Golden Pillar of Society

**Ikeda:** I believe that a life dedicated to advancing with a pioneering spirit is noble and worthy.

President Wahid, history will always honour you as the first democratically elected president of Indonesia. You have fought long and hard for democracy. I am sure that you must feel deeply gratified at this trailblazing achievement.

Are there any world leaders to whom you look up as models?

**Wahid:** The leader in history who impresses me the most is the third US president Thomas Jefferson. The reason is that he taught that the people of America possessed basic rights – in other words, human rights.

**Ikeda:** Yes, I see.

Jefferson, one of the founding fathers of American democracy, is a figure in whom I also had a great interest from my youth.

Just as you say, Jefferson dedicated himself to the struggle for human rights.

He was proud to have penned not only the Declaration of Independence but also the famous Virginia Statute of Religious Freedom.

It was only after World War II and the adoption of a new constitution, that religious freedom was finally guaranteed in Japan.

My mentor Josei Toda, who was persecuted by the militarist

Japanese regime during World War II, had a deep appreciation of the significance of that right.

He and I frequently discussed the life and beliefs of Jefferson, who so highly valued religious freedom.

**Wahid:** Jefferson's emphasis on the importance of religious freedom was one of his great accomplishments.

He also has another achievement of which he was rightfully very proud: education. Jefferson recognized that education is the driving force behind the growth of democracy and the foundation for the establishment of human rights.

**Ikeda:** I wholeheartedly concur.

Toward the end of his life, he established the University of Virginia. It was truly one of his greatest triumphs.

He proudly declared: 'I look to the diffusion of light and education as the resource most to be relied on for ameliorating the conditions, promoting the virtue and advancing the happiness of man.'[1]

**Wahid:** A quality education is the pillar of society and an enduring source of hope for the world. As Pramoedya wrote: 'Such an honourable character is the result of a good basic education. It is such an education that gives rise to good deeds and actions.'[2]

**Ikeda:** Yes, education nurtures people. People nurture peace, culture, and prosperity.

You succeeded the laudable educational endeavours undertaken by both your grandfather and father, expanding their scope and further developing them, and in this way fostering many capable individuals.

For my part, I have also inherited the spirit of our founder Tsunesaburo Makiguchi and our second president Josei Toda, both of whom were educators, and have chosen education as my life's crowning undertaking.

Soka University of America (SUA), which I founded in 2001, will soon be celebrating its tenth anniversary. I offered the university four guidelines: (1) Foster leaders of culture in the community; (2) Foster leaders of humanism in society; (3) Foster leaders of pacifism in the world; (4) Foster leaders for the creative coexistence of nature and humanity.

Many bright young people from more than forty countries, including

Indonesia, are studying at SUA, and five classes have already graduated and begun to actively contribute in various fields.

It is still a young school, but it has already earned high marks and hopes from educators around the world as a liberal arts college that offers a sound humanistic education.

Numerous luminaries in a wide range of fields, including the Nobel Peace laureates Dr Joseph Rotblat (1908–2005) and Betty Williams, as well as former ambassador Anwarul K. Chowdhury, have visited the campus and delivered lectures and addresses to our students.

Meeting outstanding individuals when you are young is an unsurpassed form of spiritual and intellectual sustenance.

The olive tree honouring you and your wife that we planted in front of the guest reception centre at SUA has grown into an outstanding specimen.

I hope that someday we can welcome your family there.

**Wahid:** Thank you. I am profoundly grateful for your warm friendship.

The four guiding principles of Soka University of America are indeed exemplary.

The key to the relationship between education and the purpose of life, I believe, when viewed in perspective, is in finding a balance between morals and material imperatives. A balance is needed for finding true happiness in life.

Education is not just a matter of academic learning. An exclusive focus on the pursuit of learning will only lead to confusion.

In other words, education must produce individuals who are useful members of society. This is, I think, a common feature of the *pesantren* schools and Soka education.

**Ikeda:** You are indeed widely known for your focus on the education of the whole person. A life dedicated to education bears the mantle of eternal glory.

What is it that governs the balance of which you speak? I believe it is the wisdom to make full use of the knowledge and learning one has acquired for the sake of others and society.

It goes without saying that the acquisition of knowledge is an important part of education. But knowledge alone does not create value; knowledge, after all, can be put to both positive and negative use.

My mentor used to say that one of the great fallacies of people today is that they confuse knowledge with wisdom.

Wisdom, in a certain sense, is part and parcel of one's way of life. It is indivisible from our capacity for tolerance or compassion.

Education must cultivate the self-discipline to never found one's happiness on the unhappiness of others. It should also foster a sense of purpose, of mission, of responsibility to seek one's own happiness by contributing to the happiness of others.

Which is why I imparted this query to students of Soka University in Japan many years ago: 'For what purposes should one cultivate wisdom? May you always ask yourself this question!'

**Wahid:** I firmly believe that our sense of social responsibility must be proportionate to our degree of learning, and I have striven to ensure that this was so in my own life.

I pledged to follow the examples of my grandfather and father in this respect, and embody that principle in my own life as well.

My grandfather and father had a very heightened awareness of the importance of social morality. I see their way of life as an embodiment of the principle called *kiai kampung. Kampung* means village or settlement, and *kiai* is an Islamic teacher.

In other words, *kiai kampung* means Islamic instruction to teach how we can develop our moral nature and make exemplifying that ideal our duty in daily life, in the community.

From my days of attending the *pesantren* I remember my grandfather's great uprightness of character and elevated moral behaviour, offering an example to all. He achieved that state of being through his highly developed quality of tolerance.

Just as you say, those who lead a life embodying tolerance can never become people who have lost their moral sense.

**Ikeda:** Your grandfather was a great educator. I have long been convinced that every educator should have a teacher who earns his or her respect and who serves as an example to emulate.

Lomonosov Moscow State University, with which we at Soka University have carried on academic exchanges for many years, looks up to its founder, the brilliant Russian scientist Mikhail Lomonosov (1711–65), as a model.

Lomonosov declared: 'Let us build a palace of learning there! And ignorance will pale in its presence! The truth will give us victory.'

The Russian aristocracy, out of their arrogance, persecuted the eminent scientist because he longed to build a university for the common people. Though he was the one who laboured hardest to establish the university, he was not even allowed to attend its opening ceremony or to teach there.

But his spirit as the founder was faithfully inherited by his protégés and passed on to later generations.

I will never forget what the university's present president, Victor Antonovich Sadovnichy, said: 'Overseas guests often ask me why our university is named after a man who has never taught here. We are named after Lomonosov, I tell them, because we are the inheritors of his ideas, and nothing is more potent than the power of ideas.'

In addition to your father and grandfather, which other educators do you admire?

**Wahid:** One great educator I admire whom I would like to mention is Ki Sarino Mangunpranoto (1910–83), who served as Indonesia's Minister of Education and Culture. He studied under Ki Hajar Dewantara (1889–1959), who founded the Taman Siswa educational movement.

The greatness of the founder has resulted in equally great successors.

When Ki Sarino lived in Semarang (on the north coast of Central Java), I often met him at seminars and on other occasions.

He taught me how to cultivate a fine moral sense and to focus on the development of society.

He was a dear friend, and he established an agricultural college.

**Ikeda:** The Tawan Siswa schools that Ki Hajar Dewantara established played a pioneering role in the education of the Indonesian populace and are well known for the important contribution they made to the development of your national culture.

I have heard that the Indian poet and playwright Rabindranath Tagore (1861–1941) visited the schools, and educational exchanges were established between them and the school Tagore founded.

**Wahid:** Yes, that's true. Ki Hajar Dewantara's birthday, 2 May, is Indonesian National Education Day.

He regarded education and culture as the most effective weapon against the Dutch colonial regime of the day and a central rallying

point for the people's spirit, which led him to establish schools to provide education and help the Indonesian people develop.

Before Indonesia's independence, it was Ki Hajar Dewantara
who first employed the word 'Indonesia'. After he was banished by
the Dutch in 1913, he started a news service called 'Indonesische
Persbureau' (Indonesian Press Bureau).

The word 'Indonesia' was then adopted in the 1920s by activists for
Indonesian independence.

To me, the name Indonesia has profound political connotations,
embodying the identity of our people carrying out their struggle for
independence.

Ki Hajar has said: 'We must not forget that the independence of
our people, and our political independence, are not sufficient in themselves. A people's independence must also mean that they have the
ability and the power to establish the independence of their culture.
In other words, the uniqueness and identity that we possess essentially and entirely, rooted in an era of expansive, noble, and profound
humanity.'[3]

Speaking of the importance of education rooted in the life of the
people, he also said: 'Children need to be familiar with the life of
the people, so that they do not only acquire knowledge about the lives
of the people but can experience it personally and thus lead lives that
are not divorced from those of the people.'[4]

**Ikeda:** He raises a very salient point.

Culture is an expression of human life, the existence and livelihood
of the people. As a result, we become firmly rooted as human beings
through the transmission of our cultural heritage. From our heritage,
we learn the models that have been prized by many others in our culture and reinforce our connections with other people.

Many in Japan are concerned that as the trend toward urbanization
intensifies, local culture, rooted to the community, is declining.

The great German educator Friedrich Wilhelm August Fröbel
(1782–1852) wrote:

Nothing inspires children, boys, and young people with a true feeling
of strength, with the sure and vibrant feeling of an elevated spiritual
life, more effectively than complete familiarity with their immediate
environment and the region in which they were born and have lived,
knowing in detail about their natural environment and its products, and
having a complete understanding of them. Nothing has the function of

reinforcing the true feeling of strength, of reinforcing and fostering the sure and vibrant feeling of an elevated spiritual life, as the awareness of this feeling.[5]

This is a core element of humanistic education.

Tsunesaburo Makiguchi, the founder of Soka education, observed in his *A Geography of Human Life* (1903) that the most important means for shaping children into responsible and creative members of adult society is to allow them to learn about life and culture by personally interacting with their environment and local region.

Today in Brazil, a major initiative based on Mr Makiguchi's educational theories is underway. It began in 1994, and more than a million children are now involved.

With the slogan, 'Competition in Creativity, not Memorization!' the initiative, with the cooperation of parents, the community, and schools, aims to provide young children with hands-on educational activities allowing them to share experiences and learn in a freer, unstructured manner.

For example, as part of their class on gardening they grow vegetables, make sandwiches with the vegetables they harvest, and serve them to family members who come to observe their classes.

By raising vegetables, they learn that fostering living things requires a great deal of thought and manifold steps. As they watch their family members enjoying the vegetables they have grown, they also derive a sense of satisfaction and enjoyment.

Learning by doing, they discover how a single vegetable is connected to human beings, nourishes our lives, and can foster ties among human beings.

**Wahid:** That sounds like a very interesting class. What the students learn in that way will certainly cultivate practical wisdom that will enrich their lives.

Previously I heard that Mr Makiguchi endorsed the importance of learning through experience, while also stressing the need for lifelong education, enabling people of all ages to continue learning throughout their lives.

As a matter of fact, there are no age restrictions at our *pesantren*, either. Not only children and teens, but adults study there as well. Some of them use the sacred month of Ramadan to engage in studies. I personally teach at two *pesantren* during the month of Ramadan.

My strong impression of education at present, based partly on my experience at the *pesantren,* is that young people are eagerly seeking inspiring models in life.

This links up to what I said earlier – that we need to provide our youth not just with education but also actual human models that can serve as examples and guides.

In other words, the most pressing problem for Indonesian youth today is that they have lost such models to emulate.

**Ikeda:** You yourself, President Wahid, have served as an exemplary model for youth. But what you say applies equally to Japanese youth as well.

To encounter a great individual who serves as an example in one's youth is an exceptionally fortunate thing. I know that from personal experience.

I am reminded of how the Russian literary giant Leo Tolstoy (1828–1910) encouraged a certain young person.

That young person grew up to become the renowned French author Romain Rolland (1866–1944). Struggling to reach deeper insights on life and art, Rolland wrote a letter to Tolstoy, who was moved by its contents and wrote a long letter back, responding to the unknown young man.

Rolland was so deeply moved by Tolstoy's reply that for the rest of his life he described the Russian author as his guide and mentor, ultimately writing a biography of Tolstoy to share his virtues with the world.

The year after Tolstoy's death, Rolland described his feelings: 'The life we imbibed from Tolstoy became our life, and through us, will become the life of the next generation, and the next, and the next.'[6]

There is no greater source of nourishment for young people than contact with individuals of elevated character and profound wisdom.

Which is why educators who interact with youth on a daily basis should constantly strive for their own growth as human beings and encourage their pupils from the heart.

Education comes down to educators – that is my firm belief.

In 1984, I proposed that members of the Soka Gakkai educators group record their experiences in carrying out their pedagogical activities, so that such case studies could serve as materials that could contribute to the overall advancement of education. Through the cooperation of many fine teachers, some 35,000 pedagogical records, or case studies, have been compiled. Every year educators from around Japan assemble and hold conferences at which they report on their experiences in humanistic education.

One of the central observations these case studies share is that people change people; that when educators change, their pupils change. They also show that all children possess infinite potential. They strongly bring home the point that educators are the most important factor in the educational environment.

In his teachings, Nichiren states: 'Here a single individual has been used as an example, but the same thing applies equally to all living beings.'[7]

Education is a great adventure in which the transformation of a single individual leads to the transformation of millions.

**Wahid:** The collection of such educational case studies is indeed a very valuable endeavour.

**Ikeda:** Youth is the time when we ponder most deeply such questions as the meaning of life and the purpose we should embrace as we lead our lives. The encouragement we receive from our teachers at that time can serve as a spiritual support that sustains us over a lifetime.

Education is the most serious of struggles, with life – the most sublime of all possessions – in the balance.

I have the deepest respect for teachers, who strive tirelessly for the sake of young people. I regard education as a sacred endeavour, and those engaged in it life's greatest champions. The triumph and validation of our lives rests with education, which is why our educators are truly our greatest leaders.

**Wahid:** I agree completely.

I believe that the crucial points that youth – indeed all of us – should cultivate in our lives are to be open-minded, honest, and dedicated to the public good. These are my three mottoes.

Many people profess to accept these as their guidelines in life, but in far too many cases they only pay them lip service.

I have always believed I must put them into practice and act as a model for others in those three respects.

My long-cherished wish has been to establish a new horizon where all people are equal before the law, free from discrimination because of the colour of their skin, their race, or their religion or beliefs, and that society should be tolerant of all teachings and political orientations.

I feel keenly that fostering young people who will shoulder the future of a peaceful, new Indonesia, free from prejudice and hate, is indispensable to realizing that goal.

Unfortunately, there are too few people in the world who possess that peaceful and tolerant spirit.

**Ikeda:** Tolerance is a core virtue that education should cultivate. It is founded on empathy and respect for the lives of others.

We find precious cultural and spiritual traditions wherever we look, in every place or country.

At a time when militarism was the predominant mode of thought in Japan, my elementary school teacher once spoke to us in class of the great treasure house of Buddhist art in Dunhuang, China, introducing us to a love of the great cultural legacy of the rest of Asia. Eventually the interest he sparked in me as a boy came to fruition when I engaged in a discussion with the painter Chang Shuhong (1904–94), known as 'the guardian of Dunhuang'.

We must never forget the history of Japan's brutal invasion of China, Indonesia, and many other Asian nations.

The magnificent cultural heritage that is the vibrant product of the human spirit is the treasure of all humanity, transcending differences of ethnicity, race, religion, or political boundaries. Education needs to cultivate an attitude of actively seeking to learn, with an open mind, from that common legacy.

The Japanese poet Matsuo Basho (1644–94), who received enormous artistic inspiration and nourishment from Chinese literature, taught his own disciples that one never stops learning.

Your favourite author Mochtar Lubis was enchanted by the expression of human emotions found in Basho's poetry. He wrote that though he would never forget the brutal and inhumane actions of the Japanese military during the war, he also learned 'the human face' of the Japanese from the haiku poetry he read in his youth.

He also cited one of Basho's poems teaching Japan the role it should play in Asia:

Deep autumn;
My neighbour,
How does he live?[8]

I find myself deeply moved by this sincere question, as well as the regard Lubis had for Japanese culture.

Unless it develops harmonious ties with Indonesia and every other Asian country, the future of Japan is indeed bleak.

**Wahid:** I believe that we need to expand our amicable and cooperative relations in education and many other areas for the sake of the peace and growth of Asia.

Japan is one of Asia's leading and most developed nations.

The changes and sudden growth taking place in Japan have exerted a powerful influence in Asia and the rest of the world.

Today Indonesia is facing the issue of its role in an ever more complex world. I think the same can be said for Japan.

One of the challenges facing Indonesia is the need for the countries of the Association of Southeast Asian Nations (ASEAN) to demonstrate the initiative that led Japan in its amazing growth.

It is thought that Japan needs to play a role in aiding and supporting the other Asian nations in moving in a positive direction.

In other words, friendship must not stop at amicable relations. This is an extremely important point, I believe.

The reason is, we need to guard against allowing ourselves to become prisoners of our self-interest, but rather give priority to our common interests.

**Ikeda:** I am of the firm belief that to build a foundation for lasting peace in Asia, we must surmount the entrenched barriers of national interest and cooperate on a regional basis, while building trust and confidence among the region's nations.

In December 2005, the first East Asia Summit was held in Malaysia, with leaders from the ASEAN nations, as well as those from Japan, China, Korea, India, Australia, and New Zealand, taking part.

In the peace proposal I issued the following month, I called for the holding of regular dialogues among leaders of the region and the establishment of an agency to concretely promote regional cooperation.

As a tangible first step in this new direction I suggested that the region should adopt initiatives to confront common threats that transcend national borders, proposing cooperation in three specific areas: public health and disease prevention, such as strategies for dealing with new flu outbreaks; the promotion of collaborative reconstruction efforts, taking the earthquake and tsunami of Sumatra as a lesson; and programmes to prevent environmental destruction and pollution.

**Wahid:** Yes, those are all urgent problems.

To overcome them, I think the most important factor in working with people of other nations is unity of purpose.

It must be a unity based on respect for social diversity, in which all nations respect the unique features of the other's cultural traditions.

**Ikeda:** As you say, without mutual understanding, efforts to work together will not yield outcomes that most people will be content with.

Yet, if such efforts are not linked to the facilitation of mutual understanding, then the gains will remain fleeting and fail to contribute to trust building.

To avoid this pitfall and deepen understanding between countries, I believe we need to promote exchanges between common citizens, particularly among the younger generations.

With regard to this point, I have previously referred to the Erasmus Programme (European Community Action Scheme for the Mobility of University Students) and similar initiatives that have been adopted in Europe, and suggested that a programme to broaden educational exchanges between the youth of Japan and East Asia be established.

I have devoted myself to educational exchange over the years in the belief that active exchange and the building of friendships among youth, the men and women who will shoulder the future, will create an unassailable foundation for peace.

When I visited China for the first time, in 1974, a Japanese journalist asked me what I regarded as the most pressing issue between our two nations.

Though official diplomatic relations had finally been restored between China and Japan, this was before the Sino-Japanese Peace Treaty had been concluded.

I promptly replied that exchange between our young people was an overriding priority, creating opportunities for those who will shape our collective future to interact.

When I visited China again six months later and met with Zhou Enlai, then premier of the People's Republic of China, our discussion focused on building enduring friendship between our two countries that would continue from generation to generation.

The following year, 1975, Soka University became the first Japanese university to accept officially accredited exchange students from China since the normalization of bilateral relations. I personally acted as the students' guarantor, and I welcomed them warmly, with Premier Zhou's fond recollections of his time as a foreign student in Japan firmly in mind.

Since then, some 1,500 students and teachers have visited Soka University from China or gone from Soka University to study or teach in China. Moreover, in 2006, Soka University opened a branch office in Beijing.

**Wahid:** That is a wonderful record of accomplishment. I think it is a very significant programme.

**Ikeda:** The Soka Gakkai youth division is also deeply involved in exchange programmes with the All-China Youth Federation (ACYF), to which more than 370 million Chinese young people belong.

Our youth division has sent eleven delegations to China, and sixteen delegations from China have visited Japan.

I first proposed this exchange between the Soka Gakkai youth and the ACYF when I visited China in 1984. The following year, a young Hu Jintao, who would later become president of China, arrived in Japan as the leader of the first delegation, and an exchange agreement between the two groups was signed.

On that occasion, Hu Jintao stated his resolve to work together with Soka Gakkai youth for the sake of a splendid future between China and Japan.

In 2008, thirty years after the signing of the Treaty of Peace and Friendship between Japan and the People's Republic of China, I was reunited with then President Hu Jintao and we discussed the importance of young people.

At that time he imparted a message to the youth of Japan: 'The seeds of friendship sown in youth are everlasting.'

We, too, are determined to sow as many seeds of peace and friendship as possible in the hearts of youth. They blossom with immeasurable splendour over time and bear rich fruit.

**Wahid:** Japan and China are two of the major nations of Asia.

Events occurring between them have a major influence on the growth and situation of East Asia.

From that perspective as well, if the ideas you have proposed and the efforts in which you have taken the initiative to open the way are expanded upon and result in more harmonious relations between China and Japan, they will act as a fresh breeze bringing increased stability to the East Asian region.

**Ikeda:** You are a great pioneer in dialogues between civilizations in your own right. Cherishing your warm encouragement, I will continue in my efforts.

Presently Soka University has exchange programmes with over 100 universities around the world, half of them in Asia.

I am delighted and honoured to be able to say that exchange programmes with the University of Indonesia and other schools in your country are also working out well.

Sunaryo Kartadinata, president of the Indonesia University of Education, who has visited Soka University twice, has spoken of the importance of instilling in society the values of peace and humanity and remarked that good values are imparted from generation to generation through education.

In addition, Indonesia's National Education Minister Muhammad Noeh, when he was president of the Institute of Technology Surabaya (ITS), also identified with our goals. He said that the best and shortest route to world peace, though at first it may seem like the long way around, is to seek the things we share in common, rather than attacking one another over our differences, and to treat one another with mutual respect.

An extensive network of education for the promotion of peace and tolerance is growing between Indonesia and Japan.

Education is the eternal light leading to humanity and peace.

I hope we can extend new bridges of friendship built by the youth of our two nations by further broadening opportunities for educational exchange – for the sake of Asia's progress in the twenty-first century, and for peace.

# EIGHT

# The Vital Roles of Women and Youth

**Ikeda:** In 2009, Soka University was honoured to welcome delegates from the University of Indonesia, followed by a group of teachers from the Indonesian Association of Private Higher Education (APTISI).

I'm told that their visit led to a very meaningful exchange of ideas on such topics as the challenges that private universities in Japan are facing as a result of a falling birth rate, and operating a university based on its founding principles.

The principles on which private universities are established are what animate them.

The founding philosophy of Soka University is represented by the following mottoes: (1) Be the highest seat of learning for humanistic education; (2) Be the cradle of a new culture; (3) Be a fortress for the peace of humankind.

Dr Sutarno, vice rector of the Islamic University of Indonesia, is among the educators who heartily approved of our school's founding spirit, relating that his university also upheld the ideal of peace and was striving to advance its cause.

I am delighted that educational exchange between the young people of Soka University and Indonesia is ongoing.

**Wahid:** Dr Sutarno chose to visit Soka University from among all the many private universities in Japan. That demonstrates, I believe, the deep trust and high appraisal in Indonesia of the university you founded.

Exchange between Indonesian universities and Soka University is growing year after year.

**Ikeda:** Your friendship has been a crucial factor in this development.

I'm told that when the teachers of APTISI learned of our meetings through photographs that were on display in an exhibition at Soka University, they were delighted and broke out in spontaneous applause.

The occasion served as an opportunity for our faculty and students to reaffirm their respect for you, having seen for themselves how revered you are by your compatriots.

**Wahid:** You are too kind.

Once when I visited Soka University I said that democracy must rest upon a foundation of spirituality, of morality.

Soka University has demonstrated a model for action in society, and the university also practises morality in its education. I am very aware of this.

**Ikeda:** Thank you for your understanding of our school.

After visiting Soka University, the APTISI teachers viewed the exhibition 'Glory of the Habsburg Empire – Palaces in Austria' at the Tokyo Fuji Art Museum.

Prof. Dr Ir. Budi Santoso Wignyosukarto described being deeply inspired in being able to appreciate in person some of these great European artworks.

One of the precepts of the Hapsburg dynasty, which commanded a large area of Europe from its seat of power in Austria, was 'The harp is more powerful than the sword', and its rulers were strong benefactors of culture.

You are also a great supporter of culture, and are especially fond of music. Is there any musical piece from or related to Vienna that you particularly favour?

**Wahid:** Yes. I am especially fond of the works of Mozart performed by the Vienna Philharmonic Orchestra under the direction of Seiji Ozawa.

During World War II the pianist Lili Kraus (1903–86), who was renowned for her performances of Mozart, visited Indonesia on one of her world tours. She taught at the Vienna Music Academy.

The Hapsburg monarchy supported both Mozart and Beethoven.

In addition, many great musicians flocked to Vienna to take part in the music culture of the city.

This was not only because of the Hapsburg support for art, but also, I believe, because of the spirit of tolerance that existed there.

**Ikeda:** Lili Kraus is famous in Japan as well. During World War II, when she played in Indonesia, she was apprehended by the Japanese imperial military and interned in a concentration camp in Indonesia until the end of the war.

In any age or place, the spirit of tolerance is the cradle for the creation of great art. It is a key quality of our humanity that must be preserved by all means.

The Austrian author Stefan Zweig (1881–1942) remarked: '"Live and let live" was the famous Viennese motto, which today still seems to me to be more humane than all the categorical imperatives.'[1]

Zweig underscored the need to accept and to live in harmony with different peoples and cultures, and saw mutual coexistence and prosperity as principles that were vital to cultural innovation.

I believe this is a quality underpinning Indonesian culture as well.

**Wahid:** Yes, you're right. Indonesian culture possesses the ability to absorb external challenges and cultural influences.

As the poet Amir Hamzah (1911–46) noted, the arrival of Hinduism, Buddhism, and Islam in Indonesia was accompanied by the cultures that gave rise to those religions. Indonesian culture developed by absorbing those cultures as it grew.

**Ikeda:** The history of religious and cultural tolerance in your country offers a shining example to the world.

In 1781, the Austrian monarch Joseph II (1741–90) issued the Patent of Tolerance, in which he declared his belief that 'all violence to conscience is harmful.'[2]

The patent recognized the right of Lutherans, Calvinists, and Greek Orthodox believers to practise their religions freely and affirmed their full rights as citizens of the empire. It also extended to followers of Judaism.

The religious tolerance that Joseph II and his successors supported was expanded to include followers of Islam.

Dr Felix Unger of the European Academy of Sciences, with whom I engaged in a dialogue, spoke proudly of that fact.

Furthermore, Article 19 of the Austrian Constitution, adopted in 1867 during the reign of Emperor Franz Josef I (1830–1916), stated in part: 'All the races of the state shall have equal rights, and each race shall have the inviolable right of maintaining and cultivating its nationality and language.'[3]

The defining principle of Emperor Franz Josef I's reign was unity and cooperation. He pursued a path that would allow the various peoples making up his empire to work harmoniously together. History reveals just how difficult this was to achieve.

In Asia, Indonesia is known for realizing unity in diversity, demonstrating the wisdom and practice of enabling some 300 peoples to coexist harmoniously and serving as a model for humankind.

**Wahid:** In the end, it is the practice of the virtue of tolerance that serves as the main force for achieving unity in diversity.

As a fellow human being and as a citizen, I have respect for every member of society.

We must put an end to the history of cruelty, darkness, and intolerance. By breaking through the barriers of outmoded ways of thought, we must build a new paradigm.

**Ikeda:** That is an important observation of which the leaders of our world should take note.

The word 'diversity' reminds me of the traditional Indonesian dyeing technique batik, which produces fabrics of manifold colours and patterns.

In one of his books Mochtar Lubis observed that 'Human life is rich and varied, it's like a woven fabric with multi-coloured designs.'[4]

Up to the end of the nineteenth century, the technique of resist dyeing on plain cloth did not exist in Europe. Advanced Indonesian dyeing techniques and designs thus had a major influence on Europe.

**Wahid:** Yes, that's true. Batik, a legacy of the royal court culture of Java, was included in UNESCO's Intangible Cultural Heritage list in October 2009.

Previously the Indonesian shadow puppet theater *wayang kulit* and the beautifully wrought traditional dagger, the *kris*, had received that designation.

This has reinforced the appreciation of the art of batik.

**Ikeda:** Batik has spread around the world, including Asia, Europe, and Africa, where it has been adopted in various ways in accord with local customs.

According to my research, batik arrived in Japan in the eighteenth century. Known as *jawa sarasa* (Javanese printed cotton), it still remains popular, being employed in the obi sash for kimono and other traditional uses.

**Wahid:** Batik is a form of traditional culture that has long linked Indonesia and Japan.

Traditional culture is intimately linked to people's lives.

In former times, when going on a long journey, it was customary to visit one's parents wearing batik and make a formal farewell greeting.

I think that Indonesia and Japan have a similar culture of respecting the elderly, but recently this attitude is being diluted to a degree.

Even so, the essential spirit remains alive. I think that 'respect' is a keyword linking Indonesia and Japan, with pluralism as the foundation.

**Ikeda:** That's an important point. When we respect others, we in turn are respected.

It's interesting that a significant movement that helped to open the way to Indonesia's independence had strong ties to batik.

I am referring to the Javanese Batik Traders' Cooperative, the Sarekat Dagang Islam, established in 1911 by batik merchants. I'm told it later evolved into the Islam Cooperative, Sarekat Islam, becoming the first genuine grassroots movement in modern Indonesia.

Abdul Muis (1886–1959), the leader of Sarekat Islam, was exiled for his criticism of colonial rule, yet he persisted in his literary activities and social activism based on firmly held convictions. A line in one of his novels says, 'Human beings must strive. It is wrong to do nothing and leave matters in the hands of fate.'[5]

It is certainly true that without Herculean effort nothing great can be achieved.

A remarkable event in modern Indonesian history took place on 28 October 1928.

On that date, even though they were aware that the authorities may try to suppress them, 750 young people from all over Indonesia gathered at the Indonesian Clubhouse in Jakarta for the historic Indonesian Youth Congress II, which became a foundation for independence.

This gathering, which took place the year I was born, will never be forgotten.

**Wahid:** The development of the movement for Indonesian nationalism, starting with the founding in 1908 of the first political society for Indonesians, Budi Utomo, shifted into the direction of a struggle for independence with the adoption of the Youth Pledge at the Indonesian Youth Congress II.

The Youth Pledge declared: '1. We the sons and daughters of Indonesia, acknowledge one motherland, Indonesia. 2. We the sons and daughters of Indonesia, acknowledge one nation, the nation of Indonesia. 3. We the sons and daughters of Indonesia, respect the language of unity, Indonesian.'

This historic national event did not immediately create an Indonesian people. It was necessary to overcome many differences – of ethnicity, religion, race, and class – in order to achieve the shared objective of independence.

October 28, the day of the Indonesian Youth Congress II, is now celebrated as Youth Pledge Day, an opportunity to remember and celebrate the inception of our independence movement.

For Indonesians today, the Youth Pledge is a reminder that we are one people, with one language, and one country. It brought together all the many and diverse peoples of Indonesia.

**Ikeda:** The fact that young people from throughout the country, with differing languages, histories, and cultures, were able to pledge to unite as a single force holds great significance as an expression of the principle of unity in diversity.

Moreover, I understand that the Indonesian Clubhouse, where this historic event transpired, was a lodging where young people, with their gaze firmly set on the future, regularly met to study the history of revolutionary movements in the world and discuss what should be done.

History is not made under the limelight. The tide of historical change emerges from wherever young people, inspired by high ideals, congregate.

Today the SGI is engaged in extensive exchange with the Indonesia Youth Conference, with its illustrious tradition. We are honoured to do so.

**Wahid:** It is also an honour for Indonesia.

**Ikeda:** The Youth Pledge states 'We the sons and daughters of Indonesia', clearly affording equal treatment to the sexes.

Women have played an extraordinary role in the history of Indonesia, haven't they? For example, the legendary Queen Shima of the Kalingga kingdom, who was praised for her impeccable integrity.

There is also Queen Ratu Gayatri (1272–1350), who played a key role in overcoming the turmoil and uncertainty in the early years of the establishment of the Majapahit kingdom. It is said that the kingdom's prime minister Gadjah Mada was able to govern effectively because of the protection and support he received from Queen Ratu Gayatri.

In Austria, which we discussed earlier, Empress Maria Theresa (1717–80), lovingly known as the mother of the kingdom, successfully carried out the reforms needed to modernize the realm.

Austrian pioneer of European integration Richard Coudenhove-Kalergi, with whom I engaged in dialogue, cited the example of Empress Maria Theresa, among others, when he argued that the idea that men make better leaders than women is just an unfounded prejudice.

There are several heroic female figures in the history of Indonesia's courageous struggle against foreign domination, such as Martha Christina Tiahahu (1800–18) of the Maluku Islands, and Cut Nyak Dhien (1848–1908) from Aceh.

In the first half of the twentieth century, the great women's movement in Indonesia drew the attention of women working for peace around the world.

Raden Ajeng Kartini (1879–1904) is particularly well known in that context, isn't she?

**Wahid:** Yes, Kartini died at the age of 25, but in addition to being a pioneering figure in the Indonesian women's movement, she is admired by many in Indonesia for her role in our struggle for independence.

Her grandfather, Condronegoro IV, was the first Indonesian to offer Western education to both his sons and daughters alike.

Kartini's father followed in Condronegoro IV's footsteps and sent all his children to school.

But, because of the feudal customs that prevailed at the time, his daughters were unable to continue their education beyond the elementary level, and were forced to stay quietly at home until they were married.

This led Kartini to question why women were forced to live such a life, deepening her thinking.

**Ikeda:** I've learned that Kartini was inspired with renewed courage and hope when she read in the newspaper about the actions of Pandita Ramabai (1858–1922), a woman educator who was reaching out to help the poor and uneducated women of India. As Kartini would write:

> I remember it still so well; I was very young, a child of ten or eleven, when, glowing with enthusiasm, I read of her in the paper. I trembled with excitement; not alone for the white woman is it possible to attain an independent position, the brown Indian too can make herself free.[6]

**Wahid:** Yes. And then Kartini courageously stood up and devoted herself with the greatest enthusiasm to expanding educational opportunities for women.

The home has the greatest role to play in education. As such, Kartini wanted to provide the light of education to future mothers in the hope of seeing them fulfil their mission as the most outstanding educators.

Kartini was certain that awakened women would exert a powerful influence on society. From her teens, it was her dream to be active as a teacher of women. She wrote:

> I should be so glad, so happy, if I could be in a position to lead children's hearts, to form little characters, to awaken young minds, to help to mould the women of the future who will be able to carry forward enlightenment like a torch. There is much misery in our Javanese woman's world, there has always been so much suffering, so much bitterness.[7]

Kartini faced criticism and opposition, but she remained true to her noble dream and, the year before her death, she founded a small private academy for girls.

Her educational ideals were carried on after her death, and her own Kartini Schools, as well as many others like them, were established throughout the country.

**Ikeda:** The story of Kartini's youth – dedicating oneself to one's mission and transforming one's personal sufferings into the power to impart hope to others – is a spiritual legacy of inestimable worth that encourages women in Asia and throughout the world to this day.

I have employed Kartini's words and accounts of her life on numerous occasions to encourage young women in Japan. My hope has been to inspire them with Kartini's message that their courage has the power to change society and the course of history.

**Wahid:** Thank you for making the example of a woman who is the pride of Indonesia better known to others.

**Ikeda:** At about the same time that Kartini was blazing a trail for the education of women in your country, the founder of Soka education, Tsunesaburo Makiguchi, was also making an effort to expand educational opportunities for women in Japan.

In his major work *Soka Kyoikugaku Taikei* (The System of Value-Creating Pedagogy), Makiguchi held that the nature of motherhood is 'the original educator' and the creator of the ideal future society.

**Wahid:** Makiguchi's words resonate powerfully with Kartini's beliefs. What efforts for the education of women did Mr Makiguchi make?

**Ikeda:** In 1904, the last year of Kartini's life, Mr Makiguchi was teaching at a private girls' school.

The discriminatory attitude that women didn't need an education prevailed in Japan at that time. For both economic reasons and because of the dearth of educational facilities, most women could not receive an education beyond the elementary level.

Out of concern for the plight of women, and firmly believing that education was indispensable to their independence, Mr Makiguchi established a variety of programmes for them.

To mention just one, in 1905 he established the Dai Nippon Koto Jogakukai (Great Japan Women's High School), a pioneering institution in correspondence-course education for women, of which he was the director. It offered women who had completed their elementary education but, for a variety of reasons, were no longer able to attend school, the opportunity to complete their studies. Mr Makiguchi also composed some of the lectures that were included in the curriculum.

For women without any education, who could not attend school, he also cooperated in the establishment and operation of tuition-free centres that taught various skills, such as dressmaking and crafts.

**Wahid:** I can see that Mr Makiguchi dedicated himself to women from all walks of life, responding appropriately to their respective needs.

**Ikeda:** For the next twenty years or so, he was an elementary school principal. In that role, he proved himself to be a compassionate educator who made the happiness of pupils his first priority.

For example, on snowy days he would wait outside the school gates to greet students, carrying little children into the school on his back and taking the hands of the older students and leading them inside. He even prepared boxed lunches for children who couldn't afford to bring their own lunch from home.

He composed *Soka Kyoikugaku Taikei* while working as an educator, drawing on the practical experience he accrued. In the foreword to the book he wrote:

> When I think seriously about these matters, I have to admit to myself that the results of this line of thinking may not be realized in my lifetime. Nonetheless, I have come to burn more and more with a fever to do something – and the sooner the better – about the deplorable state of the nation's education. Just the thought that through this effort might possibly come the difference in saving our million or more students from entrance difficulties, 'examination hell', unemployment, and other contemporary neuroses has brought it all into focus for me.[8]

**Wahid:** It was also Kartini's wish to reduce the sufferings of children and all people and make their lives wonderful.

Her unshakable conviction was that women had the greatest capacity to advance the welfare of the human race.

She wrote: 'One of the precepts which I wish to inculcate is this: honour every living creature, respect their rights, their feelings; and even when it seems necessary, shrink from causing the least suffering to another.'[9]

**Ikeda:** Her words communicate the depths of her compassion and why she strove to protect and nurture all life.

The sanctity of life is indeed fundamental to humanistic education.

Mr Makiguchi, who lovingly cared for his pupils as an educator, began to deepen his view of life by exploring the philosophy of life's sanctity articulated in the Lotus Sutra.

The Lotus Sutra represents what can be described as a declaration of the rights of women, upending prejudices against women by expounding the principle of gender equality.

Somewhat of an aside: women authors of some of the masterpieces of classical Japanese literature – both Murasaki Shikubu (978–1014 or 1025), who wrote the *The Tale of Genji*, the world's oldest novel, and

Sei Shonagon (966–1017 or later), author of *The Pillow Book* – were well versed in the Lotus Sutra. Shonagon, in fact, cited the Sutra as one of the most important Buddhist sutras.[10]

**Wahid:** That's a very interesting historical fact.

**Ikeda:** I believe one of the things we seek from religion and philosophy today is their capacity to inspire and draw forth the potentialities innate to women.

To return to our subject, I am especially struck by Kartini's refreshingly open-hearted, accepting attitude, and the way she took delight in discovering that people of other countries, ethnic backgrounds, or customs shared her thoughts and sentiments.

She was an early advocate of the idea that 'when the outstanding customs of one people are combined with those of another, that combination engenders better and more wonderful customs',[11] looking to a future when this might happen.

No matter how outstanding something is, it cannot continue to develop in isolation. In fact, it is only by actively seeking out what is new and different that further growth and eminence can be achieved.

I was also very impressed by the process in which Kartini came to be aware of the beauty and distinction of her own culture, vividly embodied in the Indonesian people. She wrote, for example: 'Oh, I hear so much wisdom and truth from the mouths of the people, and it is expressed in such sweet, melodious words.'[12] She also declares:

> But go around with me into Kampong and Dessa; let us visit the small huts of the poor submerged tenth, let us listen to their speech, seek out their thoughts. They are an unschooled people always, but music comes welling from their lips; they are tender and discreet by nature, simple and modest. If I am ever with you I can tell you much of our gentle people; you must learn to know and love them as I do. There are so many poets and artists among them, and where a people has a feeling for poetry, the most beautiful thing in life, they cannot be lacking in the instincts of civilization.[13]

Indonesia is most certainly gifted with an exalted artistic tradition.

Rather than thinking the grass is always greener elsewhere, those who can find pride and satisfaction in their own community and society are happy. This is because they are expressions of our own lives, inseparable from ourselves.

And in our exchanges with others, we rediscover and are reawakened to our own culture.

**Wahid:** Exactly.

Kartini's thought and life became known and transmitted clearly to the present in the form we know today when her friend J. H. Abendanon (1852–1925) collected Kartini's letters to her friends and published them in 1911 as *After Darkness, Light Is Born*.

Abendanon carried out her work without seeking any financial remuneration, and he used all the royalties from the book's sales to build Kartini schools around the country.

The publication of *After Darkness, Light Is Born* introduced Kartini's ideas to a broader public, later playing a role in the movement for the improvement of women's status and the Indonesian Awakening movement.

Publication is a very important means for transmitting thought to subsequent generations.

**Ikeda:** It certainly is.

My mentor Josei Toda also founded and operated publishing companies.

In addition, at the age of twenty-three – about the same age that Kartini opened her school – Mr Toda established a private academy, Jishu Gakkan, to put Makiguchi's educational theories into practice.

It was also through the efforts of Toda, Makiguchi's closest protégé, that *Soka Kyoikugaku Taikei* was published.

It was released during the darkest hours of the Great Depression.

With Japanese society in chaos, Makiguchi decided it was time to unfurl the banner of Soka education and open the way to the happiness of all children.

Toda embraced his mentor's spirit as his own and volunteered to assemble and edit the enormous amount of material that Makiguchi had collected to publish *Soka Kyoikugaku Taikei*, taking full responsibility for financing its publication as well.

**Wahid:** That must have been extremely difficult in the very midst of the global depression.

**Ikeda:** As you can well imagine, raising the necessary funds was an onerous task.

But the success of the Jishu Gakkan and Toda's self-published *Deductive Guide to Arithmetic* – which sold over a million copies – provided Toda with earnings that he used to publish his mentor's masterwork, while he personally compiled and edited the book.

The first volume of the work, an embodiment of the shared spirit of mentor and disciple, was published on 18 November 1930.

Reflecting on those times, Toda confided that while no one aside from Makiguchi had ever praised him for his unseen toils, the satisfaction he knew in his heart was irrepressible – words that remain with me to this day.

Today, we celebrate the publication of the first volume of *Soka Kyoikugaku Taikei* as the anniversary of the establishment of Soka Gakkai, imbuing the date with great significance in terms of the mentor and disciple relationship.

**Wahid:** In Indonesia, 21 April, Kartini's birthday, is celebrated throughout the country as Kartini Day, commemorating her thought and her life.

In addition, in 1964 she was officially designated a national heroine, and her image was once portrayed on the 10,000 RP note.

**Ikeda:** That attests to how much she is loved and respected by the Indonesian people.

In Japan, too, ever since her collected letters were translated into Japanese in 1940, the number of people who have come to know of her beliefs and noble life has been growing.

In 1963, the year before she was designated a national heroine in Indonesia, Japan sent your country a statue of Kartini as a gesture of friendship.

**Wahid:** Yes, I am happy to hear that.

I would like to share some of the words of Kartini with young people, as a form of encouragement. First: '"He who does not dare, does not win" is my motto. Forward! Dare mightily and with strength. Three-fourths of the world belongs to the strong.'[14]

Second, I offer a passage that I once copied out to rouse my own spirits: 'Go, work for the realization of your ideals; work for the future, work for the good of thousands who are bent beneath the yoke of unjust laws, who have a false conception of good and evil. Go suffer and fight. Your work will be for all time!'[15]

**Ikeda:** Those are stirring words, indeed. They express the essence of the spirit of youth.

What message would you like to impart to young women, President Wahid?

**Wahid:** There are many important things I'd like to say, but I think that what you stressed earlier, continually asking oneself about the purpose of one's studies, one's work, and one's life, is essential.

In other words, they should never forget that they are studying, working, and living for the sake of others.

In Indonesia, the women's movement has continued since Kartini's day, and women have gone on fighting for their rights, so that, whether men like it or not, many doors in society have opened to women and they have won new opportunities for themselves.

It is important for society to preserve those opportunities for women, to enable their further advance. At the same time, women need to fully meet the responsibilities that are entailed by the rights that they have gained.

To young women I would say, don't forget the history of your struggles for equality up to now, and no matter how far you advance in your career or what status you attain, continue to dedicate yourself to the welfare of society and other people.

**Ikeda:** Those are all very meaningful points.

In September 2009, the United Nations underwent structural reforms that constitute a trend I believe is worthy of note.

Four UN groups working for women, including the United Nations Development Fund for Women and the Division for the Advancement of Women, have been merged to create a more dynamic and better-funded group.

I have long called for UN reforms that focused on the importance of women.

While the UN is promoting the empowerment of women who are living under harsh circumstances around the world, I believe that by opening the way to greater participation by women in various UN activities, a broader and more varied spectrum of opinion will be reflected in UN policies across the board, and help usher in a bright new age for the UN.

In that context, I welcomed the 2009 UN reform as one befitting the institution in the twenty-first century.

In recent years, public agencies engaged with the issues involved in improving the status of women have been established in many countries around the world. Indonesia was one of the first Asian countries to have a government ministry for the advancement of women.

**Wahid:** Yes. Indonesia has a Women's Empowerment Ministry.

Dr Meuthia Farida Hatta Swasono is the minister. She is the daughter of the first Indonesian vice president, Mohammad Hatta (1902–80), who was a good friend of my father.

The Women's Empowerment Ministry originated from the establishment of a cabinet minister for women's issues in 1978, following the 1975 International Women's Day.

That means that the improvement of the status of women became one of the basic policies of the Indonesian government more than three decades ago.

In addition, the National Council of Women of Indonesia, a federation of women's groups that operates as a non-governmental organization (NGO), has existed and been active for more than fifty years.

Mrs Sulasikin Murpratomo, who was Minister for Women's Affairs under the Suharto administration, was a leader of the NGO and a personal friend, who often visited my home.

In 1995, the Fourth World Conference on Women was held in Beijing, and representatives from countries around the world assembled for the cause of women's rights. Mrs Sulasikin Murpratomo contributed to that conference in various ways.

**Ikeda:** 'Women's empowerment' was a key phrase at the Fourth World Conference on Women.

At around that time, a symposium was held following the Beijing conference at the Boston, Massachusetts-based Ikeda Center for Peace, Learning, and Dialogue, which included reports on the conference.

In addition, many representatives of the women's and young women's divisions from Soka Gakkai attended an NGO forum held in Beijing just prior to the conference.

For many years, women in Soka Gakkai in Japan have played a leading role in the effort to build a peaceful society. From 2002, the exhibition 'Women and the Culture of Peace' was held at venues nationwide, and since 2003 Soka Gakkai women's division members have sponsored 'Culture of Peace' forums.

Peace scholar Dr Elise Boulding (1920–2010), who curated the exhibition 'Women and the Culture of Peace', sent the following words of encouragement on its opening day: 'The important thing is to develop women's inherent strength and gentleness on a wide scale throughout local communities.'[16]

In Indonesia there is a saying describing an arduous effort: 'Like sowing seeds on stone.' There are a multitude of women in the world who are engaged in the incredibly challenging effort of serving their children, their families, and their societies, under the harshest of circumstances and criticism.

Earlier we spoke of the efforts of your wife Mrs Shinta Nuriyah over the years to improve the status of women. Your daughter is also working for an NGO committed to women's issues, isn't she?

**Wahid:** Yes, my second daughter Yenny took part in NGO activities for farming women when she was a graduate student. Today, as the director of the Wahid Institute, she is supporting my activities in various ways.

**Ikeda:** She has been of great help to the SGI as well.

In 2008, when a delegation from our organization visited Indonesia, she welcomed them warmly as the director of the Wahid Institute. I'd like to take this opportunity to reiterate my appreciation.

I understand that she continues to play a growing role in world affairs, having been selected as a participant in the Forum of Young Global Leaders of 2009 announced by the World Economic Forum (WEF).

**Wahid:** Thank you.

My daughter was delighted to meet with the SGI delegation.

**Ikeda:** I am very much aware of her activities to promote in society the spirit of tolerance and respect for diversity that you advocate.

In an interview, she shared the following insights:

The main mission of the Wahid Institute is to establish the message of peace as the core of Islam, and we are engaged in a variety of activities to reinforce that message. Around the world today Islam is often associated with certain extremists, who give the impression that Islam is a religion of hatred, a religion of terrorism, a religion of violence. This is not right, and we want to reestablish peace as the core message of Islam.[17]

Both my wife and I were very moved to hear that.

**Wahid:** I am very grateful for your understanding of the activities of our institute.

I established the Wahid Institute in 2004 to promote religious cooperation and cultural pluralism, and we have been actively engaged in the promotion of dialogue among different religions and cultures, as well as in publication projects.

I am of course profoundly aware of the pioneering role you have played in such activities, President Ikeda.

In recognition of your trailblazing efforts and your contributions to world peace over many long years, in 2008 our institute presented you with a special award.

At the presentation ceremony, Yenny, speaking as the institute's representative, recognized you as a model practitioner of the philosophy of humanism, noting the importance you have accorded dialogue as a means to resolve problems arising between different cultures. She also cited your establishment of a network for peace through your publication activities and confirmed the institute's wish to work together with you in solidarity in dealing with the many problems our world faces.

The presentation ceremony was covered by Indonesia's leading newspaper, *Kompas*, as well as the English-language *Jakarta Post*.

**Ikeda:** Yes, I'd like to reiterate my gratitude for all that you have done. I regard having received this award from the Wahid Institute, an eminent Indonesian organization for promoting peace, as an unsurpassed honour and source of joy.

Promoting dialogue among religions and civilizations is indeed one of the most pressing issues in our troubles times.

Recently the Toda Institute for Global Peace and Policy Research, which I founded, sponsored an international conference at Soka University on the theme of 'The Power of Dialogue in a Time of Global Crisis'.

At the conference, University of Tunis El Manar Prof. M'hamed Fantar said that since the crisis we face is global in nature, and the danger a collective one that threatens the entire human race, no single person can live alone, meaning that one could not possibly build a lifeboat exclusively for oneself.[18]

He called for the engagement of dialogue among peoples, civilizations, cultures, and religions – dialogue founded upon good faith and respect toward the interlocutor, whoever he or she may be and wherever he or she may be. Our duty, he said, is to ponder deeply this planetary crisis. He remarked that the problems seem to demand an ethical and moral resolution which, along with its religious dimension, also includes political, economic, social, and cultural considerations.[19]

I believe that the dialogue we must seek today is one that, even in the darkest night, when it seems the light of hope and idealism is lost, will serve as a torch to illuminate not only our own surroundings but those of others, enabling us to join hands and take that one step forward.

It is my deeply cherished wish to work together with the people of Indonesia, for whom I have the highest respect, to further add to this far-reaching groundswell of dialogue as we set forth toward building a global society of genuine peace and harmonious coexistence.

# Afterword by Daisaku Ikeda

A book can lead to a new encounter.

A key reason why this dialogue with the unforgettable Abdurrahman Wahid, the eminent Islamic leader and former president of the Republic of Indonesia, came to be was because he had read my dialogue with the English historian Arnold J. Toynbee.

When Dr Toynbee and I were about to conclude our discourse, which took place over a two-year period in his London apartment, he expressed his hope that I, who was forty years his junior, would initiate a wave of dialogue that serves in bringing the world closer together. I also recall how deeply he admired and appreciated Indonesia, its history as well as its culture.

Which is why my heart grows fonder for both President Wahid and Dr Toynbee, who I am sure would be delighted by the publication of this dialogue in the UK.

President Wahid strove tirelessly for the welfare and well-being of his people, wisely advancing the causes of human rights, democracy, and respect for diversity in Indonesia, a great nation with a population of more than 200 million. His exceptional leadership is a vivid manifestation of courage, the pillar of genuine tolerance, for fearlessly accepting that which made others different; of an unshakable commitment to the worth and dignity of all human beings; and of a compassionate love for each person and all people.

The opening year of the twenty-first century was rocked by the 9/11 terrorist attack on the United States. My discussions with President Wahid, which began the following year, arose from our shared belief that humanity needed to return to the task of realizing peace, the point from which all human endeavours must begin. We were united in our conviction that human happiness is the true purpose of religion, and that all religions, whatever differences might be found among their teachings, can cooperate in the interests of peace for all humankind. Like old friends, we were able to discuss Islam and Buddhism freely and openly, discovering a clear and certain light of hope we may convey to younger generations.

When I asked President Wahid to offer a message to young people, his response was: 'Open your heart and act with honesty.'

How are we to overcome the narrow-minded intolerance that underlies war and conflict? How can we broaden the bonds of our humanity that unite us? In this work, President Wahid lucidly cites the philosophy of peace and wisdom of tolerance as solutions.

His insights offer an invaluable guide and inspiration in advancing dialogue among religions and civilizations that is certain to become the increasing focus of humankind.

The final chapter of our free-flowing dialogue is titled 'The Vital Roles of Women and Youth'. Shinta Nuriyah Wahid, the president's soulmate, life companion and beloved wife, has embraced and carried forward her husband's work to foster the power of women and youth, uniting them, as we describe in the chapter, in the task of creating a new era of peace and harmonious coexistence. In this she has been joined by the entire Wahid family and the members of the Wahid Institute and the Nahdlatul Ulama (NU).

The profound understanding and heartfelt support of Mrs Wahid and the Wahid family, along with the members of the institute and NU, have equally been instrumental in seeing this dialogue to fruition. I express my deepest gratitude and appreciation to each and all.

While lecturing at Soka Women's College, Shinta Nuriyah Wahid encouraged her young listeners in the spirit so wonderfully embodied by her husband, saying that women in the twenty-first century are meant to lead lives of triumph.

Every member of the human race, transcending differences of ethnicity, culture, and religion, was born into this world to secure happiness not only for themselves but for others as well. A united movement of conscientious global citizens will certainly choose the path of peace, friendship, and harmonious coexistence, refusing to succumb to and inevitably prevailing over every form of violence, prejudice, and disparity. That the paean to the victory of human life will ultimately resound throughout the future of our global society – I joined President Wahid, a great educator in humanity, as we shared this common cause, exploring its depths and offering our prayers for its realization. Our belief in this will never waver.

My heartfelt hope is that this work – which is infused with President Wahid's stirring call assuring us of that victory in the years to come – will, in turn, spawn further encounters like ours, inspiring others with renewed hope.

In closing, I would like to express my sincere gratitude to Iradj Bagherzade, Chairman and Publisher of I.B.Tauris & Co. Ltd, and to all of you involved in the publication of this book.

Daisaku Ikeda
16 March 2015

# Notes

## Chapter One

1  Arnold Toynbee and Daisaku Ikeda, *Choose Life: A Dialogue* (Oxford: Oxford University Press, 1976).

2  In his book, Toynbee stated 'In this, the two world religions of Jewish origin, Christianity and Islam, have been the worst offenders; but Hinduism, and even Buddhism, have not been guiltless. It is therefore remarkable, and encouraging, to find three of these religions living together amicably in Indonesia today.' See Arnold Toynbee, *East to West: A Journey Round the World* (Oxford: Oxford University Press, 1958), p. 49.

3  Arnold Toynbee, *East to West: A Journey Round the World* (Oxford: Oxford University Press, 1958), p. 50.

4  Ibid., p. 221.

5  Nichiren, *The Writings of Nichiren Daishonin*, trans. Soka Gakkai (Tokyo: Soka Gakkai, 1999), p. 4.

6  W. Woodvukke Rockhill, *Udanavarga: A Collection of Verses from the Buddhist Canon* (London: Trübner & Co., 1883), p. 31.

7  A motto from Johann Schiller, *Wilhelm Tell* (Pennsylvania: The Pennsylvania State University, 2001), p. 24.

8  Romain Rolland, *Beethoven* (London: Kegan Paul, Trench, Trubner and Co., 1919), p. 80.

9  Ibid.

10  Pramoedya Ananta Toer, *This Earth of Mankind*, trans. Max Lane (Melbourne: Penguin Books Australia, 1982), p. 72.

11  See Abdurrahman Wahid, 'God Needs No Defence', in *Abraham's Children: Liberty and Tolerance in an Age of Religious Conflict*, ed. Kelly James Clark, (New Haven: Yale University Press, 2012), pp. 213–18.

## Chapter Two

1  The leading Japanese scholar of Arabic Studies, Torao Kawasaki (d. 1977).

See Daisaku Ikeda, *The World Is Yours to Change* (Tokyo: Asahi Publishing Company, 2012), p. 39.

2 Daisaku Ikeda, *The World Is Yours to Change* (Tokyo: Asahi Publishing Company, 2012), p. 51.

3 One of the instances of praise for knowledge in the Islamic tradition attributed to the Prophet Mohammed.

4 Barack Obama, 'Obama's Speech in Cairo', *New York Times*, 4 June 2009, http://www.nytimes.com/2009/06/04/us/politics/04obama.text.html.

5 Ibid.

6 Daisaku Ikeda and Austregésilo de Athayde, *Human Rights in the Twenty-First Century* (London: I.B.Tauris, 2009), p. 79.

7 Daisaku Ikeda and Majid Tehranian, *Global Civilization: A Buddhist–Islamic Dialogue* (New York & London: British Academic Press, 2003), p. 44.

8 Nichiren, *The Writings of Nichiren Daishonin*, vol. 2, trans. Soka Gakkai (Tokyo: Soka Gakkai, 2006), p. 379.

9 'Dengyo's Sange Gakusho Shiki' (Regulations for Students of the Mountain School), in *Sources of Japanese Tradition*, ed. Wm. Theodore de Bary, vol. 1 (New York: Columbia University Press, 1958), p. 127.

10 Antoine de Saint-Exupéry, *Southern Mail and Night Flight*, trans. Curtis Cate (London: Penguin Books, 2000), p. 174.

11 *The Qur'an: English translation with parallel Arabic text*, trans. M. A. S. Abdel Haleem (Oxford: Oxford University Press, 2010), p. 314.

12 Antoine de Saint-Exupéry, *Wind, Sand and Stars*, trans. William Rees (London: Penguin Books, 2000), p. 22.

13 Ibid., p. 29.

14 Antoine de Saint-Exupéry, *Flight to Arras*, trans. William Rees (London: Penguin Books, 2000), p. 115.

15 Ibid., p. 117.

16 See Zhou Enlai, 'Speeches at the plenary session of the Asian–African conference' (19 April 1955), in *Selected Works of Zhou Enlai*, vol. 2 (Beijing: Foreign Languages Press, 1989), p. 161.

## Chapter Three

1 Yasunari Kawabata, *The Tale of the Bamboo Cutter*, trans. Donald Keene (Tokyo: Kodansha International, 1998).

2 Arnold Toynbee, *East to West: A Journey Round the World* (Oxford: Oxford University Press, 1958), p. 46.

3 Ibid.

4 Nichiren, *The Writings of Nichiren Daishonin*, vol. 2, trans. Soka Gakkai (Tokyo: Soka Gakkai, 2006), p. 809.

5 Much of the *wayang kulit* repertory is based on Indonesian versions of the *Ramayana* and *Mahabharata*. Ravana and Kumbhakarna are characters in the *Ramayana*.

6 Translated from Japanese. Sutan Takdir Alisjahbana, '*Sensou to Ai*' (War and Love), vol. 2, trans. and ed. Kenichi Goto (Tokyo: Imura Bunka Jigyousha, 1983), p. 283.

7 Daisaku Ikeda, *The Human Revolution*, vol. 1 (Santa Monica, CA: World Tribune Press, 2004), p. 3.

8 Daisaku Ikeda, *The New Human Revolution*, vol. 1 (Santa Monica, CA: World Tribune Press, 2001), p. 7.

9 Nichiren, *The Writings of Nichiren Daishonin*, trans. Soka Gakkai (Tokyo: Soka Gakkai, 1999), p. 852.

## Chapter Four

1 Raden Ajeng Kartini, *Letters of a Javanese Princess*, trans. Agnes Louise Symmers (New York: W.W. Norton & Company, 1964), pp. 136–7.

2 Ibid., p. 137.

3 Translated summary of an article that appeared in the 5 April 2002 issue of the *Seikyo Shimbun*, the Soka Gakkai daily newspaper.

4 Nichiren, *The Writings of Nichiren Daishonin*, trans. Soka Gakkai (Tokyo: Soka Gakkai, 1999), p. 1043.

5 Ibid., p. 955.

6 Mochtar Lubis, *Twilight in Djakarta*, trans. Claire Holt (Singapore: Editions Didier Millet Pte, 2011), Kindle edition.

7 Nichiren, *The Writings of Nichiren Daishonin*, trans. Soka Gakkai (Tokyo: Soka Gakkai, 1999), p. 7.

8 Ibid., p. 24.

9 *Yomiuri Shimbun*, morning edition, 29 November 2000.

10 Nichiren, *The Writings of Nichiren Daishonin*, trans. Soka Gakkai (Tokyo: Soka Gakkai, 1999), p. 579.

11 Daisaku Ikeda and Tu Weiming, *New Horizons in Eastern Humanism: Buddhism, Confucianism and the Quest for Global Peace* (London & New York: I.B.Tauris, 2011), p. 48.

12 Ibid., p. 49.

13 Ibid.

## Chapter Five

1 As reported in *Yomiuri Shimbun*, morning edition, 27 September 2009.

2 Fuad Hassan, 'Cultural Diversity and the Prospect of Peacebuilding Through Sharing a We-World', in B. N. Setiadi, A. Supratiknya, W. J. Lonner and Y. H. Poortinga (eds), *Ongoing themes in psychology and culture,* online edition. Melbourne, FL: International Association for Cross-Cultural Psychology, http://ebooks.iaccp.org/ongoing_themes/chapters/hassan/hassan.php?file=hassan&output=screen.

3 Ibid.

4 Barack Obama, Remarks at G20 Closing Press Conference, 25 September 2009, http://www.whitehouse.gov/the_press_office/Remarks-by-the-Presi dent-at-G20-Closing-Press-Conference/.

5 *Record of the Buddhistic Kingdoms*, translated from the Chinese by Herbert A. Giles (London & Shanghai: Trubner & Co., Kelly & Walsh, 2004), p. 117.

6   See *The Buddha's Last Days: Buddhaghosa's Commentary on the Mahaparinibbana Sutta*, trans. Yang-Gyu An (Oxford: The Pali Text Society, 2003).

7   I-Ching, *A Record of the Buddhist Religion as Practised in India and the Malay Archipelago (A.D. 671–695)* (Oxford: Clarendon Press, 1896), pp. 120–1.

8   Ibid., p. 212.

9   Arnold Toynbee, *East to West: A Journey Round the World* (Oxford: Oxford University Press, 1958), p. 52.

10  Pramoedya Ananta Toer, *Footsteps*, trans. Max Lane (New York: Penguin Books, 1996), Kindle edition.

11  Ibid.

12  *The Qur'an: English translation with parallel Arabic text*, trans. M. A. S. Abdel Haleem (Oxford: Oxford University Press, 2010), p. 604.

13  'Suttanipāta Pāli', http://www.tipitaka.org/eot#56.

14  Ibid.

15  *The Record of the Orally Transmitted Teachings*, trans. Burton Watson (Tokyo: Soka Gakkai, 2004), p. 200.

16  Nichiren, *The Writings of Nichiren Daishonin*, trans. Soka Gakkai (Tokyo: Soka Gakkai, 1999), p. 72.

17  *The Lotus Sutra and Its Opening and Closing Sutras*, trans. Burton Watson (Tokyo: Soka Gakkai, 2009), p. 267.

## Chapter Six

1   Arnold Toynbee, *Acquaintances* (London: Oxford University Press, 1967), p. 248.

2   David R. Slavitt and Palmer Bovie (eds), *Aeschylus, 2: The Persians, Seven Against Thebes, The Suppliants, Prometheus Bound* (Philadelphia: University of Pennsylvania Press, 1999), p. 10.

3   Arnold Toynbee, *An Historian's Approach to Religion; Based on Gifford Lectures delivered in the University of Edinburgh in the years 1952 and 1953* (London: Oxford University Press, 1956), pp. 295–6.

4   *The Qur'an: English translation with parallel Arabic text*, trans. M. A. S. Abdel Haleem (Oxford: Oxford University Press, 2010), p. 597.

5   *Dialogues of the Buddha*, part II: *Sacred Books of the Buddhists*, vol. 3, trans. T. W. and C. A. F. Rhys Davids (Oxford: The Pali Text Society, fourth edition, 1995), p. 167.

6   Translated from Japanese. Sutan Takdir Alisjahbana, '*Kaenju – Indonesia Josei, Ai no Shousatsu*' (Flamboyant – women in Indonesia and the reflection of love), trans. Misao Kimura (Tokyo: Gakuensha, 1978), p. 154.

7   Translated from Japanese translation of *Kalah dan Menang* (War and Love). '*Sensou to Ai*' (War and Love), vol. 2, trans. and ed. Kenichi Goto (Tokyo: Imura Bunka Jigyousha, 1983), p. 3.

8   *The Lotus Sutra and Its Opening and Closing Sutras*, trans. Burton Watson (Tokyo: Soka Gakkai, 2009), p. 70.

9   *The Qur'an: English translation with parallel Arabic text*, trans. M. A. S. Abdel Haleem (Oxford: Oxford University Press, 2010), p. 604.

10  Acharya Buddharakkhita, 'Metta: The Philosophy and Practice of Universal

Love', *Access to Insight (Legacy Edition)*, http://www.accesstoinsight.org / lib/authors/buddharakkhita/wheel365.html.

11  *The Lotus Sutra and Its Opening and Closing Sutras*, trans. Burton Watson (Tokyo: Soka Gakkai, 2009), p. 203.

12  Nichiren, *The Writings of Nichiren Daishonin*, trans. Soka Gakkai (Tokyo: Soka Gakkai, 1999), p. 303.

13  *Journal of the Transactions of the Victoria Institute, or Philosophical Society of Great Britain*, vol. 28, ed. F. W. H. Petrie, FGS (London: The Institute, 1896), p. 177.

14  *The Qur'an: English translation with parallel Arabic text*, trans. M. A. S. Abdel Haleem (Oxford: Oxford University Press, 2010), p. 103.

15  Ibid., p. 208.

16  Ibid., p. 65.

17  Nichiren, *The Writings of Nichiren Daishonin*, vol. 2, trans. Soka Gakkai (Tokyo: Soka Gakkai, 2006), p. 934.

18  Nicholas F. Gier, *The Virtue of Nonviolence: From Gautama to Gandhi* (Albany: State University of New York Press, 2004), p. 54.

19  'The Doctrine of The Sword', from *Young India*, Ahmedabad Wednesday, 11 August 1920, http://www.mkgandhi.org/nonviolence/D_sword.htm.

20  *Nanden Daizokyo*, vol. 11a, 137, ed. Junjiro Takakusu, quoted in Daisaku Ikeda, *A New Humanism: The University Addresses of Daisaku Ikeda* (London: I.B.Tauris, 2010), p. 169.

21  Translated from Japanese. Hajime Nakamura, *Indo shi II* (History of India), vol. 2, *Nakamura Hajime Senshu Ketteiban* (Selected Writings of Hajime Nakamura: The Definitive Edition), vol. 6 (Tokyo: Shunjusha, 1997), p. 321.

22  Ven. S. Dhammika, The Edicts of King Ashoka: An English Rendering (1993) http://www.cs.colostate.edu/~malaiya/ashoka.html.

23  Ibid.

24  Translated from the Japanese. Ensho Kanakura, *Memyo no Kenkyu* (Study of Ashvagosha) (Kyoto: Heirakujishoten, 1966), pp. 70–73.

25  Pramoedya Ananta Toer, *House of Glass*, translated and with an introduction by Max Lane (New York: Penguin Books USA, 1997), p. 62.

26  Ibid.

27  Sakiko Fukuda-Parr, 'Human Development Report 2004 – Cultural Liberty in Today's Diverse World', United Nations Development Programme, p. 22.

## Chapter Seven

1  Saul K. Padover, *Democracy by Thomas Jefferson* (New York: D. Appleton-Century Company, 1939), p. 141.

2  Pramoedya Ananta Toer, *Footsteps*, trans. Max Lane (New York: Penguin Books, 1996), Kindle edition.

3  Translated from Indonesian. Ki Hajar Dewantara, *Menuju Manusia Merdeka* (Towards Human Freedom) (Yogyakarta: Leutika, 2009), p. 214.

4  Ibid.

5  Translated from Japanese. Friedrich Wilhelm August Fröbel, *Fureberu Zenshu* (Collected Writings of Friedrich Wilhelm August Fröbel), vol. 3, trans. Masako Shoji and Toshihiko Fujii and ed. Kuniyoshi Obara and Masako Shoji (Tokyo: Tamagawa Daigaku Shuppanbu, 1997), p. 462.

6   Translated from Japanese. Romain Rolland, *Roman Roran Zenshu* (Collected Writings of Romain Rolland), vol. 39, trans. Yoichiro Yamazaki et al (Tokyo: Misuzu Shobo, 1982), p. 346.
7   Nichiren, *The Writings of Nichiren Daishonin*, vol. 2, trans. Soka Gakkai (Tokyo: Soka Gakkai, 2006), p. 844.
8   Reginald Horace Blyth, *Haiku: Summer-Autumn*, vol. 3 (Tokyo: Hokuseido Press, 1984), p. 896.

## Chapter Eight

1   Stefan Zweig, *The World of Yesterday: An Autobiography* (Lincoln, NE: University of Nebraska Press, 1964), p. 24.
2   Joseph II's Toleration Patent (1781), http://personal.ashland.edu.
3   Fundamental Law Concerning the General Rights of Citizens. The Austrian Constitution of 1867, http://www.h-net.org/~habsweb/sourcetexts/auscon.htm.
4   Mochtar Lubis, *Twilight in Djakarta*, trans. Claire Holt (Singapore: Editions Didier Millet Pte, 2011), Kindle edition.
5   Translated from Japanese translation of *Salah Asuhan* (Wrong Upbringing). Abdul Muis, *Seiyou kabure: kyouiku wo ayamatte* (Influenced by the West: Wrong Upbringing), trans. Kenji Matsuura (Tokyo: Imura Bunka Jigyousha, 1982), p. 278.
6   Raden Ajeng Kartini, *Letters of a Javanese Princess*, trans. Agnes Louise Symmers (New York: W.W. Norton & Company, 1964), pp. 177–8.
7   Ibid., p. 113.
8   Tsunesaburo Makiguchi, *Education for Creative Living*, trans. Alfred Birnbaum and ed. Dayle M. Bethel (Ames, IA: Iowa State University Press, 1989), p. xi.
9   Raden Ajeng Kartini, *Letters of a Javanese Princess*, trans. Agnes Louise Symmers (New York: W.W. Norton & Company, 1964), p. 128.
10  *See* '[195] *Sutras* – The *Lotus Sutra*. Also the *Fugen Jugan*, the *Senju*, the *Zuigu*, the *Kongō Hanya*, and the *Yakushi Sutras* and the second volume of the *Nin'ō Sutra*' in Sei Shonagon, *The Pillow Book*, trans. Meredith McKinney (London: Penguin Books, 2006), p. 184.
11  Translated from Japanese. Raden Ajeng Kartini, *Ankoku wo koete* (After Darkness, Light is Born) (Tokyo: Nisshin Shoin, 1940), p. 156.
12  Raden Ajeng Kartini, *Letters of a Javanese Princess*, trans. Agnes Louise Symmers (New York: W.W. Norton & Company, 1964), p. 179.
13  Ibid.
14  Ibid., p. 43.
15  Ibid., p. 117.
16  Elise Boulding and Daisaku Ikeda, *Into Full Flower: Making Peace Cultures Happen* (Cambridge, MA: Dialogue Path Press, 2010), p. 67.
17  'Interview with Yenny Zannuba Wahid, Yuli Ismartono, 2nd November 2007', http://www.spf.org/the-leaders/library/21.html.
18  Translated summary of an article that appeared in the 27 November 2009 issue of the *Seikyo Shimbun*, the Soka Gakkai daily newspaper.
19  Ibid.

# Index

The abbreviations AW and DI refer to Abdurrahman Wahid and Daisaku Ikeda respectively.